First World War
and Army of Occupation
War Diary
France, Belgium and Germany

18 DIVISION
54 Infantry Brigade
Bedfordshire Regiment
2nd Battalion
1 November 1915 - 28 February 1919

WO95/2042/2

The Naval & Military Press Ltd
www.nmarchive.com
Published in association with The National Archives

Published by

The Naval & Military Press Ltd

Unit 10 Ridgewood Industrial Park,

Uckfield, East Sussex,

TN22 5QE England

Tel: +44 (0) 1825 749494

www.naval-military-press.com

www.nmarchive.com

This diary has been reprinted in facsimile from the original. Any imperfections are inevitably reproduced and the quality may fall short of modern type and cartographic standards.

© **Crown Copyright**
Images reproduced by permission of The National Archives, London, England, 2015.

Contents

Document type	Place/Title	Date From	Date To
Heading	WO 2042/2		
Heading	18th Division 54th Infy Bde 2nd Bn Bedford Regt May 1918- Apr 1919 From 30 Div 89 Bde		
War Diary	Avesnes Etrejust	01/05/1918	05/05/1918
War Diary	Warloy	06/05/1918	06/05/1918
War Diary	In Reserve	07/05/1918	16/05/1918
War Diary	In The Line	17/05/1918	24/05/1918
War Diary	Wood E of Behencourt	25/05/1918	31/05/1918
Miscellaneous	A Form Messages And Signals.		
War Diary	In the Field	01/06/1918	30/06/1918
Miscellaneous	Brigade Sports	16/07/1918	16/07/1918
Operation(al) Order(s)	54th Infantry Brigade Order No. 163.	22/06/1918	22/06/1918
Operation(al) Order(s)	Addenda to Operation Order No. 163		
Map			
Miscellaneous	Appendix "E" (to Operation Order No. 163).		
Map	To Bde H.Q. V. 4. Central Left Bde.		
Miscellaneous	Stokes Mortars Arrangements		
Miscellaneous	Appendix "F" (to Operation order No. 163).		
Operation(al) Order(s)	All Recipients of 2nd Bedfords Order No. 26.	24/06/1918	24/06/1918
Miscellaneous	54th Infantry Brigade	25/06/1918	25/06/1918
Miscellaneous	All Battalions. Signal Officer.	25/07/1918	25/07/1918
Miscellaneous	To All Recipients of 2nd Bedfords Operation Order No. 26. dt. 24.6.18	26/06/1918	26/06/1918
Miscellaneous	2nd Bn. Bedfordshire Regiment.		
Operation(al) Order(s)	All Recipients of 2nd Bedfords Order No. 26.	24/06/1918	24/06/1918
Miscellaneous	2nd Bn. Bedfordshire Regiment.	24/06/1918	24/06/1918
Miscellaneous	Operation Orders. by Sqr Boness (Com) No. 7. Platoon 2nd Bedf. R.	27/06/1918	27/06/1918
Miscellaneous			
Operation(al) Order(s)	Operation Order No. 8 Platoon	27/06/1918	27/06/1918
Operation(al) Order(s)	Operation Orders No. 5 Platoon	27/06/1918	27/06/1918
Miscellaneous	Operation Orders	27/06/1918	27/06/1918
Miscellaneous	B Coy. 2nd Bn. Bedfordshire Regt.	27/06/1918	27/06/1918
Map			
Miscellaneous	Addenda and Amendments to 2nd Bn. Bedfordshire Regiment. Order No. 26.	29/06/1918	29/06/1918
Operation(al) Order(s)	Addenda to 2nd Bn. Bedfordshire Regt. Order No. 28.	29/06/1918	29/06/1918
Miscellaneous	2nd Bn. Bedfordshire Regiment.	30/07/1918	30/07/1918
Miscellaneous	Operation Order No. 31.		
Map			
Miscellaneous	Officer Commanding.	22/06/1918	22/06/1918
Miscellaneous	Programme of Training June 23rd-28th.	22/06/1918	22/06/1918
Heading	2 Bedford Rgt Vol 42 July 18		
Heading	D.A.G. G.H.Q. 3rd Echelon		
War Diary	Albert	30/06/1918	03/07/1918
War Diary	Warloy	04/07/1918	12/07/1918
War Diary	Ferrieres	13/07/1918	29/07/1918
War Diary	Franvillers.	30/07/1918	30/07/1918
War Diary	Line.	31/07/1918	31/07/1918

Type	Description	Start	End
Miscellaneous	Battalion Orders by Lieut. Colonel. A.E. Percival. DSO. MC. Commanding 2nd Battalion Bedfordshire Regiment.	01/07/1918	01/07/1918
Miscellaneous	Account of Operations at Bouzincourt Spur 30th June to 3rd July, 1918.	12/08/1918	12/08/1918
Miscellaneous	All Coys Sgt Hills	01/07/1918	01/07/1918
Map			
Miscellaneous			
Operation(al) Order(s)	2nd Bn. Bedfordshire Regt. Order No. 28.	11/07/1918	11/07/1918
Miscellaneous	Brigade Training Camp.	11/07/1918	11/07/1918
Miscellaneous	Battalion Orders. by Major. L.H. Keep. MC. Commanding 2nd Bn. Bedfordshire Regiment.	14/07/1918	14/07/1918
Map	Plan of Ceremonial Parade 26-7-18		
Operation(al) Order(s)	2nd Bn. Bedfordshire Regt. Order NO.29.	16/07/1918	16/07/1918
Miscellaneous	54th Infantry Brigade Agenda for Conference-20th July 1918.		
Miscellaneous	54th Infantry Brigade Sporting.	27/07/1918	27/07/1918
Operation(al) Order(s)	2nd Bn. Bedfordshire Regt. Provisional Order No. 30.	28/07/1918	28/07/1918
Miscellaneous	18th Div. Art.	14/07/1918	14/07/1918
Miscellaneous	18th Div. No. 32/4 "Q"	17/07/1918	17/07/1918
Miscellaneous	Boxing Competition	16/07/1918	16/07/1918
Heading	54th Inf. Bde. 18th Division 2nd Battalion Bedfordshire Regiment August 1918		
War Diary	In Field.	01/08/1918	31/08/1918
Miscellaneous	Narrative of Operations from 5th to 8th August 1918		
War Diary	In the Field	01/09/1918	30/09/1918
Operation(al) Order(s)	2nd Bn. Bedfordshire Regt. Operation Order No. 35 Appendix I	15/09/1918	15/09/1918
Map			
Miscellaneous	Message form		
Operation(al) Order(s)	Operation Order by Major E.N. Keep M.C., Commanding 2nd Bn. Bedfordshire Regiment.		
Miscellaneous	Report on Operations 18th/20th September 1918 Appendix II		
Miscellaneous	Ref Sheet 62c. N.E. & 62c N.W.	20/09/1918	20/09/1918
Miscellaneous	Report on Operations 20th/22nd September 1918 Appendix III	25/09/1918	25/09/1918
War Diary	47 Q 16 Meels	01/10/1918	31/10/1918
War Diary		01/10/1918	31/10/1918
Miscellaneous	2nd Bn. Bedfordshire Regiment. Appendix 1	23/10/1918	23/10/1918
Miscellaneous	2nd Bn. Bedfordshire Regt.	24/10/1916	24/10/1916
Operation(al) Order(s)	Operation Order by Lt. Colonel A.E. Percival, D.S.O., M.C. Commanding Wipe. Appendix II	26/10/1918	26/10/1918
Operation(al) Order(s)	Operation Order by Major L.H. Keep, M.C., Commanding Wipe, 28.10.18. Appendix III	28/10/1918	28/10/1918
Operation(al) Order(s)	2nd Bn. Bedfordshire Regiment. Operation Order. No. 36. Appendix IV.	27/09/1918	27/09/1918
Miscellaneous			
Map	To Left Bde. H.Q. V.4. Central.		
Miscellaneous	Appendix V	25/10/1918	25/10/1918
Map	France		
Heading	2nd Bedfordshire 54th Brigade November 1915		
War Diary	Field	01/11/1915	30/11/1915
Map	Intelligence Map		
Miscellaneous	2nd Bn. Bedfordshire Regiment.	04/11/1918	04/11/1918
Miscellaneous	A Form Messages And Signals. Appendix II		

Miscellaneous	A Form Messages And Signals.		
Miscellaneous	54th Infantry Brigade Administrative Instructions issued with Order No. 200.	02/11/1918	02/11/1918
Miscellaneous	2nd Battalion Bedfordshire Regiment Order No. 41. Appendix III	12/11/1918	12/11/1918
Miscellaneous	18th Division No G. 375	23/11/1918	23/11/1918
War Diary	In Field.	01/12/1918	31/12/1918
War Diary	Field	01/01/1919	31/01/1919
Miscellaneous			
War Diary	Selvigny.	01/02/1919	28/02/1919
Miscellaneous	2nd Bn. Bedfordshire Regiment.		
Miscellaneous	2nd Bn. Bedfordshire Regiment.	01/03/1919	01/03/1919
Miscellaneous	2nd Bn. Bedfordshire Regiment.		
Map	To Left Bde H.Q. V. 4. Central		
Heading	War Diary		
Map	France		

Moscow 2012

18TH DIVISION
54TH INFY BDE

2ND BN BEDFORD REGT
MAY 1918 - APR 1919

From 30 DIV 89 BDE

WAR DIARY
or
INTELLIGENCE SUMMARY.
(Erase heading not required.)

Army Form C. 2118.

Place	Date	Hour	Summary of Events and Information	Remarks and references to Appendices
AVESNES "ETREJUST"	1st		Battalion Training. Congratulatory messages received from General Birdwood (French Army).	I
" "	2nd		4.0 p.m. 19th Corps L.G.O.C. 37th Infantry Brigade. Reinforcements: 15 O.R. from the Base	
" "	3rd		Battalion Training. Reinforcements: 66 O.R. from the Base. Honors & Awards: see Appendix II.	II
" "	4th		" " " " "	
" "	5th	9.30am	Entrained at WARLUS (T.20.C.7.8.) Proceeded to CONTAY, marching to WARLOY. (AMIENS 57)	III
WARLOY	6th		Battalion relieved 2nd London Regt in Brigade Reserve. "A" Coy in Mud Row, "B" Coy in Darling Support, "C" Coy in Villa Reserve, "D" Coy in Copse Trench. Battalion H.Q. in LOUVIEVILLE. (D.11.a.O.8.)	
In Reserve	7th		Battalion in same dispositions.	IV
" "	8th		" " " " " Capt H.H. Hay. M.C. took over duties of 2nd in Command.	
" "	9th		3/8112 Sergt. T.A. Smith awarded the Military Medal.	
" "	10th		Battalion in same dispositions.	
" "	11th		" " " " "	
" "	12th		" " " " "	

Army Form C. 2118.

WAR DIARY
or
INTELLIGENCE SUMMARY.
(Erase heading not required.)

Place	Date	Hour	Summary of Events and Information	Remarks and references to Appendices
La Rescue	12.	10.0 am	Battalion H.Q. heavily shelled with 5.9's + eventually blown in. No casualties. New Batt. H.Q. at N. end of LAVENTIE.	
"	13.		Battalion in same dispositions. LAVENTIE heavily shelled all day worth sig's + Bn Hdqs. Battalion H.Q. moved to still-still W. of cemetery, when shelled there moved to Brigade H.Q. in Quarry W. of Cemetery. Battalion relieved 7th Buffs in LAVENTIE line.	V
"	14.		Lt.Col. A.E. Percival M.C. awarded the D.S.O. Capt. H.C. Browning awarded the M.C. Reinforcements: 2nd Lieut. G.A. Rowling + 52 O.R. from the Base.	
"	15.		Battalion in same dispositions.	
"	16.	8.0 am	"A" "B" "C" Coys withdrawn from LAVENTIE line to BAZEUX. "D" Coy there hours from the "B" + "C" Coys remained in position till night when relieved. Capt. A.B. McBride and R.I.V. Doake awarded the M.C. Also Capt. T. Westream (RAMC attached) awarded the M.C. 14591 Sergt A. Scott awarded the D.C.M.	VI
Ineluhie	17.	Night 17/18	Battalion relieved the 10/15th Bn Essex Regt on the left sub-sector of the right sector of the Divisional front. "B" Coy in front line, "D" Coy in support, "A" + "C" Coys counter-attack Coys. 7.0/8 Brown.	
" "	18.		Battalion in same dispositions.	VII

WAR DIARY
or
INTELLIGENCE SUMMARY.

Army Form C. 2118.

Place	Date	Hour	Summary of Events and Information	Remarks and references to Appendices
Jutadine	19th		Battalion in same dispositions. Honours & Awards: see Appendix VIII. Reinforcements:	VIII
			Lieut. W.T. Oliver Trice + 58 O.R. from Base. Chinese attack as per Appendix IX successfully carried out.	IX
	20th		Battalion in same dispositions. 15023 Sergt. J. Wralby awarded the Military Medal.	
	21st		"C" Coy relieved "B" Coy in the front line, "A" Coy relieved "D" in Support, "B" + "C" Coys. becoming counter attack companies. Reinforcements: 16 O.R. from Base.	
	22nd		Battalion in same dispositions.	
	23rd		" " " " Reinforcements: 4 O.R. from Base.	
	24th		Battalion relieved at night by 22nd London Reg.t	X
Wood E.of Bienvillers	25th		(AMIENS 17) Reinforcements: 14 O.R. from Base.	
" " "	26th		Battalion training.	
" " "	27th		Battalion absorbed by 1st & 2nd Battalions. Lieut. A.S. Hogue wounded 26-5-18. 4 O.R. killed. 23 O.R. wounded. Lieut. J.G.R. Irving. 2 O.R. wounded and remained at duty. Casualties during the Month.	

J.G. Phillips
Captain
for Officer Commanding
7 Bn. Bedfordshire Regt.

WAR DIARY
or
INTELLIGENCE SUMMARY.
(Erase heading not required.)

Army Form C. 2118.

Place	Date	Hour	Summary of Events and Information	Remarks and references to Appendices
WOOD E. of AVELUY COURT	28".		Battalion at Training and Reorganising. Temp. Sec. Lieut. L. Tyson awarded the D.S.O. 2nd Lieut. E.J. Scott awarded the M.C. 22361. Sergt. T. Breeze +18570 Sergt. Kelly. Returned awarded the D.C.M.	
" "	29".		Battalion Training & Reorganising	
" "	30".		" " " "	
" "	31".		Battalion moved to valley W. of HENENCOURT WOOD. Strength of Battalion on attaching 7th Battalion:- 40 Officers & 1500 O.R. Remaining personnel & surplus transport were sent to the Base. Lieut. Col. R.S. Percival D.S.O. M.C. commanded the Battalion from 27/5/18. Casualties since 27/5/18 :- Nil.	

H.J. Phillips
Captain
for Officer Commanding
2nd Battn. Bedfordshire Regt.

"A" Form
MESSAGES AND SIGNALS.

Army Form C. 2121
(in pads of 100).

Prefix	Code	m.	Words	Charge	This message is on a/c of:	Recd. at........m
Office of Origin and Service Instructions.			Sent		....................Service	Date...........
			At......,......m.			From............
			To................			
			By..............	(Signature of "Franking Officer.")	By............

TO WUFA

Sender's Number.	Day of Month.	In reply to Number.	AAA
* D 345	28		

Herewith copies of Observation
Device of Col. B & C
Corps and Devon London
as requested

From MO 81 (REAR)

Place

Time

The above may be forwarded as now corrected.   (Z)

Censor.   Signature of Addressor or person authorised to telegraph in his name
* This line should be erased if not required.

Army Form C. 2118.

WAR DIARY
or
INTELLIGENCE SUMMARY.
(Erase heading not required.)

Instructions regarding War Diaries and Intelligence Summaries are contained in F. S. Regs., Part II. and the Staff Manual respectively. Title pages will be prepared in manuscript.

Place	Date	Hour	Summary of Events and Information	Remarks and references to Appendices
In the Field	1st June 1918		Reference Map. SENLIS. 1/20,000 and SHEET, 62.D.	
			Battalion in Reserve in HENNENCOURT WOOD and were Counter-attack Battalion in Brigade Reserve. Companies were situated in V.26.a.	
			6 Other Ranks joined Battalion from Base.	
			2 Other Ranks Wounded.	
			2nd Lieut.P.A. Page awarded Military Cross	
			6108 Pte.F.Scripps.	
			4/7274 Pte.F.White. } Awarded Military Medal.	
			31952 Pte. A. Coles.	
			29677 Pte. J. Fretwell.	
	2nd June		Battalion in Reserve	
			2 Other Ranks Wounded.	
	3rd June.		Battalion in Reserve.	
			3 Other Ranks from Base.	
	4th June.		Battalion in Reserve.	
			1 Other Rank Accidentally wounded.	
			1 Other Rank Wounded, at duty.	
	5th June.		The Battalion (less Battalion H.Q.) relieved 8th Bn.Royal Berks Regt as Counter-attack Battalion in the Left Sub-sector.	See Append -ix I
			Battalion H.Q. relieved Battalion H.Q. of 7th R.W. Kents.	
			Captain. W.E. Aylwin. M.C. joined Battalion.	
			3 Other Ranks wounded.	
	6th June.		Battalion in same dispositions.	
			Captain. D.P. Cross to 41 C.C.S. Sick.	
			25 Other Ranks joined Battalion from Base.	
	7th June.		Battalion in same dispositions.	

Army Form C. 2118.

WAR DIARY
or
INTELLIGENCE SUMMARY.
(Erase heading not required.)

Instructions regarding War Diaries and Intelligence Summaries are contained in F.S. Regs., Part II. and the Staff Manual respectively. Title pages will be prepared in manuscript.

Place	Date	Hour	Summary of Events and Information	Remarks and references to Appendices
In the Field.	8th June.		Battalion in same dispositions. 12 Other Ranks joined Battalion from Base. 2/Lieut.(A/Major) J.P.Pitts, awarded Military Cross. 9126 Sgt.A.Cobbold. } Awarded Distinguished Conduct Medal. 8172 ; L.Hubbocks. }	
	9th June.		Battalion in same dispositions.	
	10th June.		Battalion in the Line. Draft of 3 Other Ranks joined Battalion from Base. 3/8112 Sgt.T.A.Smith awarded D.C.M. 2 Other Ranks Killed. 1 Other Rank wounded, at duty. Lieut.J.M.Glen. 2/Lieut.A.D.Greenwood. } -:- H.J.Poulter. } To Base 10.6.18. -:- G.S.Richards. } 88 Other Ranks.	
	11th June.		Battalion in Line. On night 10th/11th Battalion were relieved by 11th Bn.Royal Fusiliers & took up dispositions. The Battalion were Counter-attack Battalion.	See appendix.2.
	12th June.		Battalion in same dispositions as Counter-attack Battalion. Captain. S.G.Hague. M.C. to leave. Draft of 3 Other Ranks from Base.	
	13th June.		Battalion were relieved by 8th Bn.East Surrey Regt & after relief proceeded to V.22. Draft of 5 Other Ranks from Base.	See Appendix. ⁊3.
	14th June.		Battalion in same dispositions. 3 Other Ranks joined Battalion from Base.	
	15th June.		Battalion in same dispositions. 3 Other Ranks joined Battalion from Base.	

Army Form C. 2118.

WAR DIARY
or
INTELLIGENCE SUMMARY.
(Erase heading not required.)

Instructions regarding War Diaries and Intelligence Summaries are contained in F. S. Regs., Part II. and the Staff Manual respectively. Title pages will be prepared in manuscript.

Place	Date	Hour	Summary of Events and Information	Remarks and references to Appendices
In the Field	June 16th		Battalion in same dispositions. Details of Battalion at MOLLIENS AU BOIS (Ref. Map AMIENS, Sheet 17).	
	June 17th		Battalion in same dispositions. 7 Other Ranks joined Battalion from Base. No.19796 Cpl.B.Parles (D of Wounds 6.4.18) awarded Meritorious Service Medal.	
	June 18th.		Battalion in same dispositions. Captain & Adjutant H.C.Browning M.C.attached to 6th Northamptonshire Regiment.	
	June 19th.		Battalion in same dispositions. 7 Other Ranks joined Battalion.	
	June 20th.		Battalion in same dispositions.	
	June 21st.		On night 20th/21st the Battalion relieved 7th Buffs & 1 Platoon of 7th Queens 3 Other Ranks Killed. 2 Other Ranks Wounded. Captain L.H.Keep M.C. granted rank of Major. Captain.H.C.Browning M.C. granted rank of Major.	See Appendix 4.
	June 22nd.		Battalion in dispositions as on 21st. T/Captain.W.J.W.Colley M.C. Temp.Major dt 30.5.18.	
	June 23rd.		Battalion in dispositions as on 22nd. 3 Other Ranks joined Battalion from Base. Lieut H.E.Mudford) Lieut.H.de Burlatte) Transferred to Base and Struck off Strength.	
	June 24th.		Battalion in dispositions as on 23rd.	
	June 25th.		The 6th Bn.Northamptonshire Regt relieved the Battalion in the Left Sector of Bde.Front on night 25th/26th. 7 Other Ranks from Base. 3 Other Ranks Killed in Action., 3 Other Ranks Wounded.	See Appendix 5.

Army Form C. 2118.

WAR DIARY
or
INTELLIGENCE SUMMARY.
(Erase heading not required.)

Instructions regarding War Diaries and Intelligence Summaries are contained in F. S. Regs., Part II. and the Staff Manual respectively. Title pages will be prepared in manuscript.

Place	Date	Hour	Summary of Events and Information	Remarks and references to Appendices
In the Field	June 26th		Battalion in dispositions as on 25th.	
	June 27th.		Battalion in dispositions as on 26th. No.26539 L/Cpl. Peacock. G. awarded Croix de Guerre. 2 Other Ranks joined Battalion from Base.	
	June 28th.		Battalion in dispositions as on 27th.	
	June 29th.		Battalion in dispositions as on 28th. At 10.15 p.m. the Battalion marched to relieve 6th Bn.Northamptonshire Regt. Lieut.F.S.Lapper joined Battalion from Base.	See Appendix.6.
	June 30th		Battalion in dispositions the Line.	

30.6.18.

J.B. Kup Major for
Officer Commanding 2nd Bn. Bedfordshire Regiment.

BRIGADE SPORTS

In order that the best man in each weight represents the Brigade, the following contests will be fought:-

On THURSDAY, in the Chateau Grounds, FERRIERES:

Heavy-weights -
1.   Sgt. Pearce (Bedfords)   v   Sgt. Blake. (Bedfords)

Middle-weights -
2.   Sgt. Coxall (Bedfords)   v   Pte. Hebbington (Bedfords)

Welter-weights -
3.   Pte. Smith.E."A" Coy.(Bedfords)   v   Pte. Liggles (North'n)
4.   Pte. Mansfield (Fusiliers)   v   Pte. McRobb (Fusiliers)

Feather-weights-
5.   Pte. Bastick "A" Coy.(Bedfords)   v   Pte. Elmore (North'n)
6.   Dmr. Farrant (Fusiliers)   v   Pte. Mould (Fusiliers)

On FRIDAY, in the CHATEAU Grounds, GUIGNEMICOURT:

Heavy-weights-
    Winner of (1)   v   Sgt. Wilson. (North'n)

Middle-weights-
    Winner of (2)   v   Pte. Palmer (Fusiliers)

Welter-weights-
    Winner of (3)   v   Winner of (4)

Feather-weights.
    Winner of (5)   v   Winner of (6)

Battalions are requested to ensure that their boxers are at the above places by 5.30 p.m. each day, complete with seconds and shoes. Competitors not present will be "scratched".

16.7.18.

(Signed) J.C.M. FERGUSON. Capt.
Amusements Officer
54th Infantry Bde.

SECRET.   Copy No. 92

54th Infantry Brigade Order No. 163.

Ref.Maps :
  SENLIS 1/20,000
  and special maps
  attached.

22nd June, 1916.

1. The 54th Brigade will capture, and hold, the German front line system from W.21.d.1.7. - W.15.d.8.0.

2. The 12th Division will simultaneously capture, and hold, the line of the road from W.15.d.8.0. - W.15.a.8.4. (approximately). O.C. 2nd Bedfordshire Regt. will ensure the closest liaison with the right of 12th Division, a special party being told off to accompany the 12th Division right column.
    The O.C.Liaison party accompanying the right of the 12th Division will have the end of an enamelled wire bound securely around a short stick (so as to avoid cutting the hands). The column commander, 2nd Bedfordshire Regt., 3rd wave, will pay out from a reel, carried on the belt, sufficient wire, so as to always keep a light touch. The wire must be kept sufficiently "taut" to prevent it "sagging" into crops or long grass.

3. Chinese attacks will be carried out by 58th Division and 53rd Brigade.

4. The attack of 54th Brigade will be made at the rate of 100 yards per minute without artillery, it will be covered by a smoke barrage, put down by No.1. Special Coy. Persistent lachrymatory gas will (weather permitting) be put down on the right of the attack (vide attached map "Z").

5. The O.C. Left Group Artillery, and O.C. "B" Coy. 18th M.G.Bn., will arrange protective barrage lines, (vide attached maps and tracings "C" and "D"). They will open 10 minutes intense fire in response to an S.O.S. or call for artillery support being received from Brigade Battle Post.

6. The 54th Brigade operation will be carried out (vide attached map "A") by the 2nd Bedfordshire Regt. on the left and 6th Northamptonshire Regt. on the right. 1 Assault Coy., 3 Officers and 120 O.R. per Battalion, plus additional Lewis guns (vide map "A"), and 1 wiring, carrying, and digging Coy per battalion only will be employed.

7. Z. day will be the night of June 30th/July 1st.

8. Zero will be notified later.

9. Troops engaged in the operation will wear a 4" white band on the right arm.

10. Twenty-seven red electric torches will be issued to each battalion; these will be flashed by wiring, carrying and covering troops when coming in.

11. Forty of each colour red, white and green, Very lights, with six Very pistols, per assault Coy. will be carried.

12. Signal communications, as per attached map and appendix "E".

13. Communication trenches will be dug (vide disposition map "A").

P.T.O.

14. Troops engaged in the operation will take over the front line system on the night 29th/30th June; the 2nd Bedfordshire Regt. making an inter-Coy. relief, and the 6th Northamptonshire Regt. replacing the front line Coy. 11th Royal Fusiliers.
Details will be arranged between Commanding Officers concerned.

15. Dumps (vide disposition map "A") will be formed under Battalion arrangements on the night 28th/29th June, and the greatest care must be taken to ensure that they are carefully camouflaged. The carrying party to form the 6th Northamptonshire Regt. dump will be supplied by O.C. 11th Royal Fusiliers. Details to be arranged between Commanding Officers.

16. Dress : Assault Coys. - battle order, 1 pick to four men, 2 bombs per man, and 120 rounds S.A.A.
Six S.O.S. signals will be carried by column commanders in each assault Coy.
Wirecutters on the scale of 1 per man will be carried.
Dress : Wiring and carrying parties - rifle, bandolier, sling, water bottle, and box respirator only. Equipment will be dumped under battalion arrangements.

17. R.M.O's. 2nd Bedfordshire and 6th Northamptonshire Regts. will make full and detailed arrangements for extra bearer squads and rapid evacuation of casualties.

18. The captured trench must be consolidated, block made, wire put out; and all covering, carrying and working parties withdrawn by 2-30 a.m.

19. Direction of columns will be kept by means of tracer bullets being fired, as per attached map "A". The columns of the 2nd Bedfordshire Regt. will keep the tracer bullets on their left; those of the 6th Northamptonshire Regt. on their right. Battalion Commanders, when siting these guns, will ensure that they are securely fixed, so as to avoid any possibility of change of direction or elevation.
Drums will be filled with tracer ammunition in the proportion of 1 tracer to 4 ordinary rounds.. These guns will fire bursts of 10 rounds continuously from zero - zero plus 15 minutes.
Two guns will be established at each direction Lewis Gun station.

20. Stokes mortar arrangements vide appendix "G" attached.

21. Running up lines and direction wires will be carefully laid out under orders of Battalion Commanders concerned; these will be carried out into "No Man's Land" for 50 yards at least prior to zero on "Z" day.

22. Stealth patrols will carefully and continuously reconnoitre the enemy's front line wire up to within half-an-hour of zero.

23. On "Z" day, at zero minus 10 minutes, Battalion scouts will rapidly and silently push out under cover of the smoke, and silently cut gaps in the enemy's wire. They will carry out a drum of single telephone wire, which they will lay as they go out. They will attach this cable to the German wire, on the side of the gap.

24. Assault columns will carry each two light bridges, or blanket mats (whichever experiments prove to be the most practical), for use in crossing wire if the gap is missed.

25. The bridges will be carried by 2nd and 3rd waves left Battalion to assist in crossing hostile front and second line trenches.

26. The 11th Royal Fusiliers and 2nd Bedfordshire Regt. will clear the front line system of all other troops back as far as the MELBOURNE TRENCH line by 10 p.m. on Z. night. Protection against surprise or raids will be ensured by pushing out posts and L.G's. into "No Man's Land". (see addenda para 34)

27. The local and immediate counter-attack, which may be expected to be delivered from either, or both, Company Headquarters W.15.d.9.1. or from about 22.c.6.8. will be beaten off by the Lewis guns and fire of assault troops vide map "A".

28. It is not anticipated that a heavy counter-attack can materialize before 2-30 a.m., and then is doubtful. This will be broken up on the wire by the Lewis guns and fire of assault Coys. Additional arrangements to hold troops in close support in the event of a heavy counter-attack at dawn or dusk the following day will be issued later.

29. Special mobile charges will be carried by 3rd wave, 2nd Bedfordshire Regt., for the destruction of dug-outs in the road.

30. Battle Posts :-
    2nd Bedfordshire Regt. ... the left Battalion H.Qrs.
    6th Northamptonshire Regt.. the right Battalion H.Qrs.
    Brigade Battle Post (where all prisoners and reports
       will be sent) .... V.23.c.9.8.

31. Smoke and gas will be fired on the objectives and to the Southern flank prior to Z. day (vide map "Z"), to educate the enemy to put his gas mask on and get the gas gong going during a smoke bombardment. With these exceptions, and the normal wirecutting and harassing fire, the sector will be kept quiet, and so give surprise every opportunity of success.

32. At 2-15 a.m. the Brigade red lamp will be hoisted from the S.E.corner of the HAIRPIN, as a signal and directing light for stragglers, covering, carrying and working parties. (see addenda para 35)

                                                    L.M. Sadleir-Jackson
                                                              Brig.Gen.,
Issued at _____   Commanding 54th Infty. Bde.

    Copies to -

        No. 1. G.O.C.   12.   36th Brigade.
            2. Brigade Major,   13 to 28. O.C. 2nd Bedfords.
            3. Staff Captain,   29 to 44. O.C. 6th North'n.
            4. Signal Officer,   45 - 46.   O.C. 11th Royal Fus.
            5. Bde. Transport Offr.   47.   O.C."B" Coy.18th M.G.C.
       6 to 9. 18th Division.   48.   O.C. 18th M.G.Battn.
           10. 12th Division.   49.   O.C.Left Group RFA.
           11. 53rd Brigade.

33. Watches will be synchronised at Brigade H.Qrs. at 3 p.m.June 30th. O.C.Left Group, "B" Coy.18th M.G.Bn., O.C.Stokes Mortar Battery, and Brigade Signal Officer, will send representatives with reliable watches. A watch will be sent to Headquarters O's. C. 2nd Bedfordshire and 6th Northamptonshire Regts. by 5 p.m.

P.T.O

Addenda to Operation Order No. 163.

34. Reference para. 26.   Add -

   These posts will remain until all is quiet, when they will withdraw according to orders given in detail.   The assault Companies will pass over these posts.

35. Reference para. 32.   Add -

   O.C. 2nd Bedfordshire Regt. will be responsible for making this arrangement.

36. O.C. 2nd Bedfordshire Regt. will arrange for a prisoners collecting station in the HAIRPIN, near the Aeroplane; O.C. 6th Northamptonshire Regt. for a similar station at W.21.b.1.1. Prisoners will be taken over at these posts, and troops will return to their assault Coys.

37. The greatest precautions will be taken to at once open fire with all Lewis guns and rifles at low-flying hostile aircraft, the morning after the attack.   O.C. 11th Bn. Royal Fusiliers will establish 3 pairs of anti-aircraft Lewis guns in present NO MAN'S LAND between HAIRPIN and SWAN TRENCH the night June 30th/1st July.

38. Password NOTTING - answer HILL.

L.G. Tracer   5% Elevation   750ˣ

L.G. Tracer.
Elevation 5%.

L.G. Tracer.   5% Elevation 750ˣ

750ˣ

750ˣ   L.G. Tracer.
Elevation 5%

SECRET.

APPENDIX "E"
(to Operation Order No. 163).

SIGNAL ARRANGEMENTS.

1. Map "E" attached.

2. The forward portion of a loop W/T set, and 1 Lucas lamp, will accompany the 2nd Bedfordshire troops taking part in the operation.

3. 1 power buzzer, with 1 spare base line, and one Lucas lamp, the 6th Northamptonshire Regt.

4. The signal stations will be under an N.C.O. and will report to O.C. respective wiring parties. They will join these parties 24 hours before zero.

5. O's. C. 2nd Bedfordshire and 6th Northamptonshire Regts. will arrange respectively for lamp station to be established by zero hour, at the HAIRPIN, near Aeroplane, and in MELBOURNE TRENCH (vide map "E").

6. The signal stations accompanying the assaulting troops will establish their stations as near as possible vide map "E". O's. C. assaulting Coys. must know exactly where these stations are to be found, and all messages must be sent to these stations, which will transmit at once IN CLEAR.

7. Unless all the four signal stations are lost, or become casualties, no runners will be sent back.

8. If such a situation as envisaged in preceding para. (7) occurs, runners will go to the signal station near the Aeroplane in the HAIRPIN.

9. Messages will be sent by any signal station, whether it is the one attached to the particular assault Coy. or not.

10. Visual will be established, but only used if wireless and power buzzer break down.

11. Great care to get correct direction in setting up power buzzer base line, and W/T. loop, so as to get the correct direction, must be taken. Compasses must be carried.

12. O's. C. wiring parties are responsible for getting the signal stations to their correct destinations.

13. To facilitate opening up visual communication, signallers in MELBOURNE and the HAIRPIN will give flashes with the ALDIS Lamp until the forward station gets its direction.

14. Once the forward station is "set", the message will not be answered by the MELBOURNE or HAIRPIN stations, except to give R.D. or ask for corrections, on account of being in full view of the enemy.

15. A steady rate of sending will be observed; messages must be as brief as possible, e.g.-
    1st objective gained.
    11-5 a.m.
is sufficient. Preamble will be cut out. Time will always be sent. Addresses to and from are unnecessary as that is known, except in the case of communication with 12th Division, which must be looked out for.

P.T.O.

16. The ordinary light signals will be used, in addition to the S.O.S. and will be repeated by all light signal stations and confirmed, and direction in which seen at once reported by signal.

17. (a). 1st objective gained.)
       2nd   do.) Succession of white very lights.
       3rd   do.)

    (b) Artillery and M.G. support required. Succession of green Very lights.

    (c) Lengthen barrage. .... Succession of red lights.

    (d) Artillery and M.G. cease fire. .. Succession of white Very lights.

18. The Brigade Signal Officer will ensure that the most careful and detailed arrangements are made to ensure that signallers clearly understand their role, and that full arrangements are made as regards rations and transport of signal stores.

19. Signallers detailed for the operation will rehearse once by day, and once by night, with the troops taking part. Full equipment will be carried, and communication actually opened.

20. Extra men will be told off to help to carry the power buzzer apparatus, and spare men to pick up the apparatus should any signaller become a casualty.

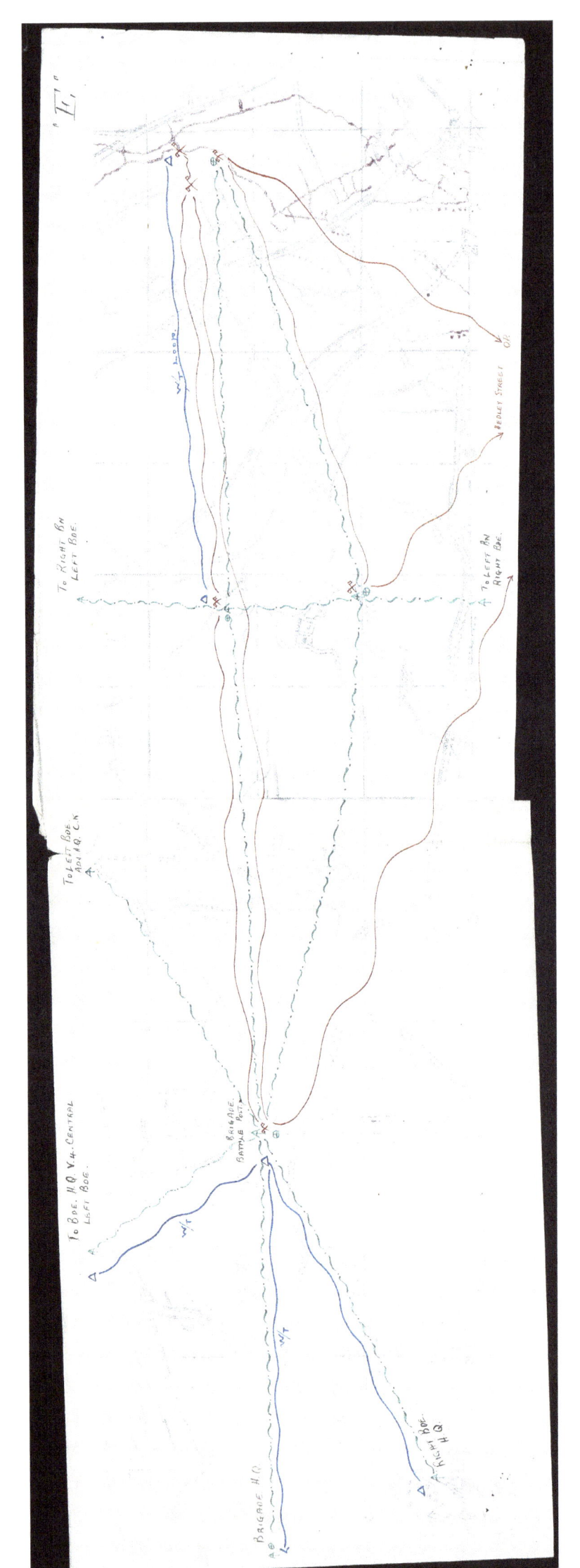

SECRET.

APPENDIX "G"
(to Operation Order No.163).

STOKES MORTARS ARRANGEMENTS.

(1). Position gun emplacement.   W.21.c.40.45.
     No. guns ....   Two.
     Target ....   M.G. at W.21.d.3.2.
     Rate of fire ....   Rapid.
     Duration of fire ....   Zero to zero plus 2 minutes.
     Fuze ....   "Always".

(2). Position gun emplacement.   W.21.c.40.45 (alternative bedplate positions).
     No. guns ....   Two.
     Targets ....   W.21.d.15.20. (1 gun).
                              W.21.d.00.15. (1 gun).
     Rate of fire ....   2 rounds per gun per minute.
     Duration of fire ....   Zero plus 5 to zero plus 60 minutes.
     Fuze ....   "Always".

(3). Position gun emplacement.   W.21.b.35.40.
     No. guns ....   Two.
     Target ....   M.G. at W.22.a.10.75.
     Rate of fire ....   Rapid.
     Duration of fire ....   Zero to zero plus 2 minutes.
     Fuze ....   "Always".

(4). Position gun emplacement.   W.21.b.10.95.
     No. guns ....   Two.
     Target ....   M.G. at W.15.d.95.05.
     Rate of fire ....   Rapid.
     Duration of fire ....   Zero to Zero plus 5 minutes.
     Fuze ....   "Always".

(5). Position gun emplacement.   W.21.b.10.95.
     No. guns ....   Two.
     Target ....   M.G. at W.15.d.85.10.
     Rate of fire ....   Rapid.
     Duration of fire ....   Zero to zero plus 5 minutes.
     Fuze ....   "Always".

"S.O.S" or call for support.

	Gun emplacement.	No. guns.	Target.	Rate and duration of fire.	Fuze.
(6).	W.21.c.40.45.	1	W.21.d.15.20.	Bursts of 1 minute with	"Always"
		1	W.21.d.00.15.	2 minute intervals for	
				10 minutes in all.	
	W.21.b.35.40.	2	W.22.a.17.55.	do.	do.
		2	W.22.a.1.8.	do.	do.
	W.21.b.10.95.	2	W.15.d.95.05.	do.	do.

Anti-Aircraft.

(7).	W.21.b.10.95.	4	Aircraft.	Rapid.	Pistol head (4 seconds).

APPENDIX "G"
--------oOo--------

SECRET.

APPENDIX "F"
(to Operation Order No. 163).

LEWIS GUNS — giving direction and objective by means of fire with tracer ammunition.

1. The position of Lewis guns detailed to fire tracer ammunition is shown in map "A" to avoid multiplying maps.

2. The positions given on map are such that the bullet ceases to trace :-

   (a) In the case of 6th Northamptonshire Southern column at the point where the furthermost column turns to the N.W. to attack, thus bounding the limit of advance of furthermost column.

   (b) In the case of 6th Northamptonshire Northern column, it will be noticed that the fire of the L.G. is on the left of the column (not on the right as in the preceding instance). The bullet in this case ceases to trace on the objective of the furthermost Southern column, and so fixes the position of enemy trench.

3. In the case of direction of L.G. tracer fire, the bullet ceases to trace in the case of the 2nd Bedfordshire right column at the point where furthermost party should reach before attacking due N.
In the case of the left column, the bullet ceases to trace on the road, or objective of 3rd wave.

4. The greatest care must be taken to fix the L. Guns so that direction and elevation shall remain fixed. Further, in order to obtain full benefit, the guns must be sited as per map, otherwise false objectives and turning points will be marked.

PTO

TO.

ALL RECIPIENTS OF 2ND BEDFORDS ORDER NO.26.

       Orders in connection with forthcoming operations are on no account to be taken beyond Battalion Headquarters in the Line. Those addressed to O.C. "A" and "D" Companies will be retained by the Adjutant who will pass on the necessary instructions verbally.

24.6.18.   *A.W.G.Smith*   2/LIEUTENANT.
ASST. ADJUTANT for O.C. 2ND BN. BEDFORDSHIRE REGIMENT.

SECRET.

54th INFANTRY BRIGADE.

B.M.414.

APPENDIX "G" to Operation Order No. 163 is hereby cancelled, and the following substituted :-

STOKES MORTAR ARRANGEMENTS.

Gun emplacement.	No. guns.	Target.	Rate of Fire.	Duration of Fire.	Fuze.
W.21.c.45.40.	2	M.G. W.21.d.2.4.	Rapid.	Zero to Zero plus 2.	"Always".
	1	" W.21.d.15.10.	"	Zero to Zero plus 5.	"
W.21.a.9.4.	2	M.G. W.22.a.05.65.	"	Zero to Zero plus 3.	"
		" W.21.b.6.3.	"	"	"
W.21.b.05.60.	2	M.G. W.15.d.75.15.	"	"	"
	2	" W.15.d.85.10.	"	"	"
W.21.b.05.80.	1	M.G. W.15.d.50.25.	"	Zero to Zero plus 1.	"
W.21.a.95.45.	2	M.G. W.21.b.8.9.	"	Zero to Zero plus 2.	"
	2	" W.21.b.8.7.	"	"	"

PROTECTIVE FIRE DURING CONSOLIDATION (Green lights).

W.21.c.45.40.	2	W.21.d.20.20.	Burst of 1 minute, with 3	"Always".
	1	W.21.d.00.15.	minutes and 4 minutes, alternately, interval, until zero plus 60.	"
W.21.a.9.4.	2	W.22.a.2.6.	do. do.	"
W.21.a.97.42.	2	W.22.a.10.75.	do. do.	"
	2	W.16.c.2.9.	do. do.	"

S.O.S.

(To be taken up when consolidation completed signal sent up - pairs of red and green lights).

W.21.c.45.40.	1	W.21.d.15.10.	Bursts of 2 minutes, with	"Always"
	1	W.21.d.2.2.	2 minute intervals, for 10	
	1	W.21.d.5.3.	minutes.	
W.21.a.9.4.	2	W.22.a.05.65.	do. do.	"
W.21.a.97.42.	2	W.22.a.1.8.	do. do.	"
	2	W.22.a.35.90.	do. do.	"
W.21.b.05.60.	4	W.22.a.05.95.	do. do.	"

ANTI-AIRCRAFT.

W.21.b.05.60.	4	Aircraft.	Rapid.	Pistol head
W.21.b.05.80.	1	do.	do.	(4 seconds).

Captain,
A/Brigade Major,
54th Infty. Bde.

25.6.1918.

(2/Bedy)

All Battalions.
Signal Officer.

Herewith map shewing parade to-morrow and routes of approach.

All units will leave by the approach of the 2nd Bedfordshire Regt.

W.R.

Captain.
Brigade Major,
54th Infantry Brigade.

25th July 1918.

SECRET

TO ALL RECIPIENTS OF 2ND BEDFORDS OPERATION ORDER NO.26, dated 24.6.18.

SIGNAL ARRANGEMENTS.

Signal.	Meaning of signal.	By whom sent up.	By whom repeated.
Pairs of red and green Very lights sent up in succession.	Consolidation completed; all covering parties withdrawn.	Assault Coy. Commander, 2nd Bedfords.	Assault Coy. Commander, 6th Northamptons. All Light Signal Stations.

26.6.18.

2/LIEUT & ASST/ADJUTANT.
2ND BATTALION BEDFORDSHIRE REGIMENT.

SECRET   2nd Bn. Bedfordshire Regiment.

ADDENDA AND AMENDMENTS TO ORDER NO. 26.

1. Para 6 - DUMPS.
    Add 50 Lewis Gun Drums (filled) in each dump. A rear dump of 100 full drums will also be made at Battalion Headquarters W.19.b.7.3.
    These will be sent up on Transport on night 29th/30th inst under arrangements to be made by the Quartermaster. Those for the Forward dumps will be carried forward by "A" Coys special carrying party.
    Add also:- 48 Rounds White V.P.A.)
               24 Rounds Red   V.P.A.) PER DUMP.
               24 Rounds Green V.P.A.)
    These will be sent up under arrangements similar to the above.

2. Para 10.   Amend as under:-
    Above ground (by night) or via CAREY TRENCH (by day). (Note:- CAREY TRENCH is being widened for this purpose).

3. GAPS IN OUR OWN WIRE.   Will be cut by "B" Company on Z minus 1 Night.

4. TRENCH LADDERS.   Are being made by 80th Field Company R.E., and will be sent up as soon as ready. They will be placed:-
    10 in new trench W.15.d.3.0 - W.21.b.2.6.
    5 in new trench W.21.b.2.2.- W.21.b.2.4.
    5 in old front line W.15.d.4.0 - W.21.b.45.60.

5. BRIDGES.   Bridges will be placed across the front line where necessary for right and left columns. These will be placed in position at Zero by men specially detailed for this work by O.C. "C" Company. These men will be drawn from the wiring parties and will rejoin their parties as soon as the bridges are in position.

6. Para 10.   For W.20.c.4.8 read W.20.d.40.65.

7. Para 14.   Is cancelled. 4 Scouts will be attached to O.C. "B" Company to be used as Intelligence men. They should report to O.C. "B" Company forthwith and will be accommodated and rationed by him.
    The remainder will be at the disposal of 2nd Lieut: HAWARD at the Advanced Intelligence Station W.20.b.8.0.

   Para 15.:- For "Expanding Metal Mat" read "Wooden Mat". These will also be carried by the 2nd wave.

8. RATIONS:- 2 days' Rations will be issued on the 29th inst. Hot Tea in food containers will be issued to "B" and "C" Companies at 5 p.m. 30th inst and will also be issued to all Companies the following morning.

                                              A.E. Percival
                                                       Lt. Colonel
26.6.1918.   Commanding 2nd Bn. Bedfordshire Regiment.

Distributed to all recipients of Order No.26.

TO.

ALL RECIPIENTS OF 2ND BEDFORDS ORDER NO.26.

   Orders in connection with forthcoming operations are on no account to be taken beyond Battalion Headquarters in the Line.   Those addressed to O.C. "A" and "D" Companies will be retained by the Adjutant who will pass on the necessary instructions verbally.

24.6.18.   *A.W.G.Smith*   2/LIEUTENANT.
         ASST. ADJUTANT for O.C. 2ND BN. BEDFORDSHIRE REGIMENT.

SECRET   2nd Bn. Bedfordshire Regiment.   Order No.26.

Copy No. 16

24th June, 1918.

With reference to 54th Infantry Brigade Order No.165 and accompanying Maps.

----

1. The 2nd Bn. Bedfordshire Regiment will capture and hold the German Front Line System from W.21.b.85/25 to W.15.d.8/0.

2. The Assault will be carried out by "B" Company.
"C" Company will provide Covering Party and Wiring Party. Formations, objectives, and position of covering parties will be as already practised.

3. The 6th QUEENS will attack on the Left of the 2nd Bedfords. O.C. "B" Company will arrange to keep close liaison with Right Company 6th Queens at W.15.d.65.00, W.15.d.8.0 and W.15.d.9.0.

4. COMMUNICATIONS
Sergeant Hills will make all arrangements in accordance with Appendix "B". The station near the Aeroplane will be sited forthwith and emplacement made ready to take the Lamp.
Personnel selected to man forward stations will report to O.C. "C" Company by 6 p.m. 26th inst.
Runner Relay Posts will be established near the Signal Station at W.21.b.6.5 and W.20.c.9.6.

5. Communication Trench from W.21.b.8.8. to W.21.b.85.90 will be dug under arrangements to be made by O.C. "B" Company with any available men.
All wiring and carrying parties will report to O.C. "B" Coy on completion of their tasks and will be available for this work.

6. DUMPS.
Rear Dumps will be established at W.21.b.6.4., and W.21.b.4.8. Each Dump will contain:-
     50 Coils Concertina Wire.
     10 Boxes S.A.A.
     15 Boxes Grenades No.23.
     12 Shovels.
     4 Picks
     10 Tins of Water.
Forward Dumps will be established at W.21.b.80.55., and W.21.b. 85.85.

7. CARRYING PARTY
O.C. "C" Company will detail Carrying Party for the wire.
O.C. "A" Company will detail 1 Platoon of not less than 20.O.R. under an Officer to carry forward S.A.A., Grenades, Shovels, Picks, and Water from REAR to FORWARD Dumps. This Platoon will be accommodated at ZERO about W.21.c.4.9., and will start carrying forward as soon as the Barrage permits enemy

8. S.O.S. RELAY POSTS.
These will be established at the Signal Station at W.21.b.6.5. (under arrangements to be made by Sgt. Hills) and at Battalion Headquarters. Each Post will have a supply of:-
     12 "S.O.S." Rockets.
     24 White Very Lights.
     24 Green Very Lights.
     24 Red Very Lights.

9. DRESS.
In addition to the two bombs per man all men of sections detailed to make Bombing Blocks will carry six No.23 Grenades in Canvas Buckets.
Equipment of Wiring and Carrying Parties will be dumped in position of assembly.

Para 10.

Operation Order No.26 dated 24.6.18.   Page 2.

10. Regimental Aid Post will be established at W.20.c.4.8. All evacuations to here will be above ground under arrangements to be made by the M.O.

11. The Signal for covering parties to withdraw will be a Red and Green Very Light sent up together from "B" Coys Headquarters.

12. Lewis Gun Officer will arrange as soon as possible to fix the Mountings for the Guns as detailed in para 19. These must be set by Compass Bearing, great care being taken that the elevation and direction are absolutely accurate. They will be checked again on Z night. Guns will be supplied by "A" Company: Teams will consist of 2 men each. They will fire for ten minutes (not 15) and will then rejoin their Company.

13. Major KEEP will arrange to lay out forming up lines and direction wires during the Battalions present tour in the line. Old telephone wire on stakes 2 foot from the ground will be used and will be carried forward to our own wire, through which gaps must be cut.

14. 2nd Lieut. HAVARD will arrange to push out 5 pairs of Scouts into NO MAN'S Land as soon as it gets dusk on Z day, accompanied by 2 Lewis Gunners, with Patrol Lewis Guns, to be detailed by O.C. "A" Company. These Scouts must prevent any enemy patrols leaving their lines. On commencement of the Smoke Barrage they will push forward and cut the enemy's wire, if it has not been previously cut by the Bombardment. After the Assault they will report to O.C. "B" Company and will be at his disposal for communicating with his Platoons or with Battalion Headquarters.
They will carry torches, which they will flash backwards to show the front wave the gaps in the wire.

15. Each Section of the front wave will carry an expanding metal mat to assist in crossing wire.

16. Paras 25 and 26 are cancelled.

17. Headquarters of O.C. Assault Troops will be established at W.21.a.7.2. they will move forward to W.21.b.78.75. Battalion Headquarters will remain at W.19.b.7.3. 2nd Lieut. HAVARD will arrange to establish an advanced Intelligence Post with Visual or Telephone Communication about W.20.b.8.0.

18. Sgt. Hills will arrange to hoist the Brigade Red Flag at W.21.b.6.4. at 2.15 a.m.

19. Watches will be synchronised at Battalion Headquarters at 6 p.m 30th inst.

20. "A" Company will detail 2 N.C.O's and 12 men to form a Prisoners Collecting Station about W.21.b.5.5. All Prisoners will be handed over to this Station, they will be collected and sent down to Battalion Headquarters. Men of Assault Companies will return immediately to their Companies after handing over Prisoners.

21. PASSWORD - "N O T T I N G" - ANSWER - "H I L L".

22. A c k n o w l e d g e.

Lt. Colonel
Commanding 2nd Bn. Bedfordshire Regiment.

Distribution as attached.

COPIES TO:-

1. Commanding Officer.   x
2. 54th Infantry Brigade
3. O.C. "A" Company   x   (To be sent to Adjutant).
4. O.C. "B" Company   x
5. O.C. "C" Company   x
6. O.C. "D" Company   x   (To be sent to Adjutant)
7. 2nd Lieut.HAWARD.   x
8. Sgt.Hills   x
9. Quartermaster.
10. Major KEEP.   x
11. Transport Officer
12. Medical Officer
13. 6th Bn.Northamptonshire Regt.
14. 6th Bn.Queens Regt (12th Division.) x
15. File.   x
16. War Diary. x
17. -do-   x

x.   Attach copy of 54th Brigade Order No.163.

Operation Orders.

By Sgt. Bones. Commanding No. 7. Platoon 2nd Bedf. R.

1. The platoon will be organised as follows:- 1 L.G. 43 rifles 6 scouts

2. No. 7 Platoon in conjunction with No. 8 Platoon will form 1st wave of the attacking force and will take and consolidate the Bosch front line from W15D 80 - W21b 85.75

3. The platoon will form up in British front line W15D 40 - W21b 40.60

4. Nos 1 and 2 Sections will consolidate the Bosch front line as stated above.

   No. 4 Section will go up communication trench at W21b 75.75 and build bombing block at W22a 00.65

   No. 3. Section (L. Gun) will be held in reserve at W21b 9.65

5. A Section of No. 8 Platoon will build permanent block at W21b 9.65

6. At the completion of consolidation a red and green light will be fired from Company H.Q.
   No. 4 Section will then return to C. H. Q.

7. No. 6. Platoon composing 2nd wave, will pass over No. 7. Platoon and assault Bosch support line

8. No. 5. Platoon composing 3rd wave, will raid sunken road, and on completion of raid, will return to C. H. Q. through No. 3. Section.

9. Liason will be kept with the 6th Batt Queens R. W15a 80

10. C. H. Q. W21b 75.75   11. R. A. P. W20d 40.60

12. Prisoners to C. H. Q.

(Continued) Operation Orders

By Sgt J Boness (Com) No. 7. Platoon 2nd Bedf R.

(13) Signals. Red and Green on completion of consolidation
Red:- Lengthen barrage
Green. Artillery support required.
S.O.S. As issued

(14) Zero and pass-word will be notified later

J Boness Sgt.
No. 7. Platoon

27/6/18.

XVI. Lewis gun sections will carry 'Very' light pistols & white ammunition

G. L'Estrange Kerr 2/Lt
O.C. 6 Platoon
2nd Bedf.

Operation Orders No 8 Platoon

Formation
27.6.16

No 8 Platoon will form the right of the first wave of the attacking Coy. from the left the order of parties will be No 5 party L/C Murray Boyd, No 6 party L/C Houghton, No 7 party Cpl Snider, R/A party Cpl Jackson. Y party 6 Coy Lewis Gun. Z party 6 Coy Lewis Gun. 6 Coy Lewis Gun Y party will form up on left of No 5 party. Z party Lewis Gun on left of Y party.

Advance

The parties will advance in single file 5, 6, & 7 parties 20ˣ apart Y 7a & Z parties 40ˣ behind. When the leading parties cross the German wire they will move with all possible speed and at the distance of 20ˣ will carry the Objective with a rush.

Objective

The German Front line W 21 b 85/25 to W 21 b 85/65.

Attached Lewis Gun.

One Lewis Gun Z gun will take up position 50ˣ in front of German Front line and act as covering party to the wiring party. No 5 party Lewis Gun Section will take up position 20ˣ in front of German front line. Y section 6 Coy will take up

2

position 50x in front of German Front Line & give covering fire to bombing party.

Action on Reaching Objective.

No 5 party on reaching the objective will clear the trench to the left and form a bombing block of the communication trench running from W 21 b 80/65 to W 21 b 9.7. No 7a party will clear & consolidate trench. No 7 party will clear trench to the right and form a temporary bombing block till in touch with the Northamptons.

Counter Attack.

Every individual must be on the lookout for a counter attack and give the alarm on his own initiative. When giving the alarm he must give the direction from which the Counter attack is coming. Each man must have his rifle fully loaded & at full cock and Lewis Gunners must exercise great vigilance and be ready to open fire at a moment's notice.

Signals.

Single red light.   Lengthen Barrage
         green.   Artillery support
Red & Green   Covering parties withdraw

W Fielder Lt
O C No 8 Platoon

No.	Date	Time	Place
To			Place

Operation orders – No 5 Platoon.

FORMATION

No 5 Platoon will form the third wave of the attacking Coy. From the left, the order of parties will be – No 12 party, L/Cpl MINNS, No 13 party L/Cpl CURLE, No 14 Cpl BRISTON, No 15 L/Cpl WRIGHT. The C. Coy Lewis Gun Section attached to the Platoon will form up on the left of No 12 party. In the forming up trench parties of No 5 will alternate with parties of No 6 platoon.

ADVANCE.

Parties will advance in single file. A distance of 50 yards is to be kept between the 2nd and 3rd waves. On the 2nd wave reaching their objective, parties will move

From

No.	Date	Time	Place
To			Place

with all possible speed, and at the distance of 20 yards from the objective will carry it with a rush.

OBJECTIVE

The sunken road in rear of the enemy support line, from W.15.d.7.2 - the cross roads - to W.21.a.1.8 - just short of where the road is cut by a communication trench to the enemy support line.

ATTACHED LEWIS GUNS.

One L.G. section will advance with the third wave, at 10 yards distance from N°12 party. A second L.G. Section will advance with the 2nd wave. This section will be in the objective

From

No.	Date	3	Time	Place
To				Place

by the time the 3rd wave reaches it.

ACTION ON REACHING THE OBJECTIVE.

The attached L.G section on the left will at once take up a position commanding both forks of the cross-roads. No 12 party, L Cpl MINNS' L.G section will command the open ground to the front. The remaining attached L.G section, which advanced with the 2nd wave, will get into position to command any approach along the sunken road past the communication trench at N 21 a 1.8

No 15 party will proceed at once and with all possible speed to the right and clean up the sunken road for at least fifty yards past the communication trench at N 21.a.1.8, in order to relieve the right L.G section from the risk of being

From

bombed. They will then return and clean up the sunken road to the left. On their return they will make certain that the communication trench running from N 21 a.5.8 has been thoroughly cleaned up.

Nos 13 and 14 parties will start cleaning up the sunken road at the point where they enter it and work up towards the right till they meet No 15 party.

Platoon headquarters will deal immediately with the enemy Coy H.Q at N 15. d 9.1.

COUNTER ATTACKS

Every individual must be on the look out for an enemy counter attack, and give the alarm on his own initiative. When giving the alarm the direction from which the counter

No.	Date 5	Time	Place
To			Place

attack is coming must be given.
L.G. sections must exercise especial vigilance in this respect and in regard to their general protection, as the other sections are likely to be fully occupied.

WITHDRAWAL

As soon as the sunken road has been cleared of enemy, Nos 13, 14 and 15 parties will ~~at~~ withdraw down the communication trench at N.21.a.1.8. They will withdraw by parties in the order 15, 14, 13 and are to exercise great vigilance while doing so. Platoon H.Q. will withdraw last. No 12 party and the two attached L.G. sections will remain behind in the sunken road to cover the wiring party. On wiring being completed they will be recalled by a red and green light sent up simultaneously from Coy H.Q.

From

No.   Date 6   Time   Place
To   Place

They will then withdraw to positions
previously assigned to them behind
our wire.
  After withdrawal the remainder of
the platoon will be at the disposal
of O.C. Coy.

KEEPING TOUCH.
        O.C. Third wave will keep
touch with the Coy on the left —
"A" Coy 6th Queen's, but the attached
L.G. sections on the left will continue
to keep touch after platoon has
withdrawn from sunken road.
  The N.C.O. in charge of the dug-
out clearing party on the left
will be Sgt. BARNES.

LIGHTS + SIGNALS
        On reaching objective O.C. third
wave will send up a white Very

From

No.	Date	Time	Place
To			Place

light

Covering parties will be recalled by a red and a green light fired simultaneously

AID POSTS.

AID POST will be at W 20 d 40. 65.

PASS WORD.
To be notified later

W.S. Menor-Jones, Lieut

27/6/18

June 27-1916.   OPERATION ORDERS

by 2/Lieut: L'Estrange-Kerr, o/c no 6 platoon, 2nd. Bedfords.

i. No 6 Platoon will be organised as under:—

    No 8 section.   Lewis gun section
    no 9   " ⎫
       10   " ⎬ Rifle sections
       11   " ⎭ also trained & equipped as bombers.

    11a section. Lewis gun (attached from 'C' coy.)

ii No 6 Platoon will form the second wave of the attacking force. It will take & consolidate the Bosch support line from W15d 8.0 – W21 69.7

iii The second wave will form up in an assembly trench at W15 d 3.0 – W21 62.6

iv It will follow the first wave at 40 yards interval & will "leap-frog" over the first wave at the Bosch front line & assault the support line.

v. Duties of sections.   no 8 will

I.
1. enter the Bosch support line at W.15.d.8.0 & establish its Lewis gun in position to cover the left flank of the attack. A block will be built at W.15.d.8.1.

(b) no 9. will enter the second line on the right of no 8 & clear the trench to the South as far as W.21.b.9.7

(c) no 10 will proceed direct to the Bosch communication trench at B.22.a.1.8 & build a temporary block.

(d) no 11 will proceed to W.21.b.9.7 (Right of objective) & build & hold a permanent block.

(e) attached Lewis gun section will establish itself at W.22.a.10.85 & cover the right flank of the attack by fire S.E down the sunken road.

v. A white light will be fired to indicate consolidation of the Bosch support line.

vi. On a red & green light being fired from Coy. Hd. Qrs (indication completion of consolidation) the Lewis gun section at W2aa 10.85 will withdraw via cross-trenches W2a b 9.5 7.0 & take up a position in shell-holes in front of block at W2a b 9.7.

vii. After covering the withdrawal of Lewis gun team from W2aa 10.85 no 10 section will withdraw to W2a b 9.9.

viii. Platoon Hd. Qrs until completion of consolidation at W2a b 9.7. Afterwards at W2a b 9.9.

ix. Closest liason will be maintained with 'A' coy. 6th Queens at W15 d 9.1

x. Signals

    red & green - withdrawal of covering parties

    red - lengthen range

    green - artillery support

xi. Coy. Hd. Qrs. ~~W21a 72~~ W21b 78.75

xii. Prisoners to Coy. Hd. Qrs.

xiii. R.A.P. W20d 40.68

xiv. Red torches will be flashed by in-coming parties.

xv. No 5 Platoon, forming third wave, under Lieut. Oliver-Jones, will raid the "sunken road" after the second wave has reached its objective. It will return via B22a1.8

"B" Coy 2nd Bn Bedfordshire Regt

Secret.   June 27th 1918

Ref. map
Senlis 1/20,000
& special map of

1.) "B" Coy. will capture & hold the German
    trench system from W21 b 85.25 to
    W 15 d 8.0.

2.) "C" Coy will provide covering and wiring
    parties.
    Formation, objectives & positions of
    covering parties will be as already
    practised. i.e. (From left to right)
    1st wave.   No 7 platoon.   No 8 platoon
    2nd -do-   6   -do-
    3rd -do-   5   -do-
    The first wave will capture and consolidate
    German front line from W 21 b 85.25 to
    W 15 d 8.0.
    The second wave will capture & consolidate
    German support line from W 15 d 8.0
    to W 21 b 9.7.
    The third wave will clear & destroy
    dugouts in Sunken road from
    W 15 d 95.15 to W 22 a 15.75
    Direction wires will be laid into NO
    MANS LAND for at least 50 yds

3). The 6th Bn. Queens (12th Div.) will attack on the left & the 6th Northants Regt on the right.

The closest liaison will be kept with "A" Coy (right coy) 6th Queens at the following points:-
W. 15 d 65.00
W. 15 d 80
W. 15 d 90

4.) Chinese attacks will be made on right by 53rd Bde and 58th division.

5.) No 7 platoon will form up in old front line trench W 15 d 40 - W 21 b 45 60 where 5 ladders will be placed.
Nos 6 and 5 platoons in new trench W 15 d 30 - W 21 b 26 where 10 ladders will be placed
No 8 platoon in new trench W 21 b 22 - W 21 b 24 where 5 ladders will be placed

6.) Bridges over old front line will be placed in position at Zero by "C" Coy.

7.) Hdqtrs of Coy will be established at W 21 a 72 & will move forward behind

— 3 —

third wave to W 21 b 75.75
Bn. Hdqtrs will remain at W 19 b 7 3.
Advanced Intelligence post with visual
or Telephone communication about
W 20 b 8.0.

8) A communication trench with
fire bays will be dug from W 21 b 85
to W 21 b 85.90 with available
men. Wiring carrying parties
reporting to OC. Coy. on completion
of their tasks will be available
for this work

9) Dress. Battle order. One pick and
three shovels to four men, two bombs
per man, 120 rounds S.A.A.
Bombing sections six N° 23 grenades
in canvas buckets per man.
Wirecutters. One per man
Six S.O.S rockets will be carried
by column commander
Every man will wear a 4" white band on right arm

10) The attacks will be at the rate of
100 yds per minute & will be
covered by a smoke barrage.
Lachrymatory gas will (weather
permitting) be put down on the right
of the attack

— 4 —

(1) "Z" day will be the night of the June 30th / July 1st.

(2) Z ero hour will be notified later.

(3) The captured trench must be consolidated, blocks made, wire put out & all covering working parties withdrawn by 2:30 am.

(4) Direction of columns will be kept by means of tracer bullets being fired by Lewis Guns under direction of Lewis Gun Officer.

(5) The following light signals will be used in addition to the S.O.S & will be repeated by all light signal stations & direct wire at once reported by signal.

   a   1st Objective gained   } succession of
       2nd   —do—   } white Very
       3rd   —do—   } lights

   b   Artillery & M.G. support } Succession of
       required   } Green V. Lights

   c   Lengthen Barrage   red light.

   d   Artillery & M.G. fire   } succession of
       cease   } white V. Light

   e   Consolidation completed } Red & green
       all covering parties withdrawn } light from
                                         Coy. Hdqtrs

— 5 —

16) <u>Dumps</u> will be established at W 21 b 6 4 and W 21 b 4 6 each dump will contain
    50 Coils Concertina Wire
    10 Boxes S.A.A
    15 Boxes No 23 Grenades
    12 Shovels
    4 picks
    10 Tins of water
    50 full Lewis Gun drums
    48 rounds White V.P.A
    24   —   red   —
    24   —   green   —

17) <u>S.O.S. Relay posts</u> will be established at the Cunice Station at W 21 b 6 5 & at Bon Hugh. Each post will have a supply of
    12 S.O.S rockets
    24 White V.P.A
    24 Green —
    24 Red —

18) <u>Regimental aid posts</u> will be established at W 20 d 40 65

– 4 –

18) <u>Evacuations</u> by night above ground by day Carey Trench.

19) <u>Gaps in our wire</u> will be cut by "B" Coy on "Z" morn one night

20) Each section of the front & second waves will carry wooden mats for crossing enemy wire if same is not cut by artillery.

21) "A" Coy will detail 12 N.CO's + 12 men to form Prisoners collecting station at W 21 h 55. All prisoners will be handed over here + men of the coy will return immediately to their position.

22) "A" Coy will supply one Officer + 20 O.R. for carrying up S.A.A. water etc forward as soon as enemys barrage permits. They will be accomodated at W 21 c 4.9.

23) Four Bn. scouts will be attached to the Coy.

— 7 —

24) The Coy. will take over the front line system on the night 29th/30th.

25) Rations. Two days rations will be issued on 29th inst.
Hot tea at 5 pm 30th & also following morning.

26) Watches will be synchronised at Bn. Hdqrs at 6 pm. 30th inst.

27) At 2.15 am the Bde. Red lamp will be hoisted at W 21 b 6.4. as a signal to directly left for stragglers.

28) Communication. Under Sgt Weir.
Runner Relay posts at
W 21 b 6.5
W 20 c 9.6
The following will accompany the Coy.
Loops W/T set
1 lucas lamp

29) Barrage. The following are the Stokes mortar arrangements:—

— 8 —

Gun emplacement	No. Guns	Target		Duration
W.21 a 9.4	2	M.G.	W 22 a 05 65	Zero to Zero + 3
	1	"	W 21 b 6 3	— do —
W 21 b 05 60	2	"	W 15 d 75 15	— do —
	2	"	W 15 d 85 10	— do —
W 21 b 05 80	1	"	W 15 d 50 25	— do — + 1
W 21 a 95 45	2	"	W 21 b 8 9	— do — + 2
	2	"	W 21 b 8 7	— do — + 2

Protective fire (in answer to Green lights)

W 21 a 9.4	2	W 22 a 2 6	Bursts of one minute with 3 minutes & 4 minutes alternate interval until Zero + 60.
W 21 a 97 42	2	W 22 a 10 75	
		W 16 c 2 0	

S. O. S.

W 21 a 9.4	2	W 22 a 05 65	Bursts of 2 minutes with 2 minute intervals for 10 minutes
W 21 a 97 42	2	W 22 a 05 90	
	2	W 22 a 1 8	
W 21 b 05 60	4	W 22 a 05 95	

- 9 -

Anti-aircraft

W 21 b 05.60   b   Aircraft   Round
W 21 b 05.80   1   "   "

30) **Lewis Guns - Anti aircraft.** All Lewis
      Guns & rifles will at once open fire
      at all low flying hostile aircraft & its
      morning after the attack.

31). Eight red torches will be issued to the
      Coy. which will be distributed to the
      covering tangent clearing parties who will
      flash same on their return journey.

32)   **Pass - word.**   Notified later.

Amendment to para (1) plus three Lewis Guns attached

H.B. Stewart
H. "B" Coy
2". Bn. Bedfordshire Regt.

S E C R E T.　　　　　　　　　　　　　　　　Copy No　16

ADDENDA AND AMENDMENTS TO 2ND BN.BEDFORDSHIRE
REGIMENT ORDER NO.26.
-:-

Reference Map:- SENLIS, 1/20,000.

1. ASSEMBLY OF TROOPS ON Z DAY

　　At Zero Hour Troops will be disposed as follows:-
"B" Company, Right Column:- NEW TRENCH, W.21.b.4.3. to
　　　W.21.b.3.4.
　Left Column:-Company Headquarters and first wave - Old Front
　　　　Line W.19.d.45.00 - W.21.b.5.7.
　　　　2nd and 3rd Waves:- NEW TRENCH W.21.b.3.8. to
　　　　　W.21.b.3.6.
"C" Company:-Left Wiring Party W.21.b.4.3. - W.21.b.6.4.
　　　Right Wiring Party Front Line Trench between the
　　　　ladder and top of CAREY TRENCH.
　　　REPORT CENTRE:- W.21.b.6.5.
"A" Company:-(less carrying and prisoners collecting station
　　　　parties) MELBOURNE TRENCH.
"D" Company:- MELBOURNE TRENCH.
Bn.Hd.Qrs :- W.19.b.7.3.
Carrying Party (1 Officer and 20 Other Ranks) TORRENS SUPPORT,
　　　about W.21.a.3.0.
Prisoners Collecting Station Party:- Front Line W.21.b.5.6 -
　　　W.21.b.5.7.
Owing to the Trenches being under observation from the North,
the greatest care must be taken in moving into position of
assembly.　The movement should extend over a considerable
period and be carried out in small parties.　Men must be told
to expose themselves as little as possible during the movement
and to lie down at bottom of trench once in position.
　　Signal Station personnel:- W.21.b.60.45.
　　All troops to be in position by ZERO minus 30 except "C"
Coys Right Wiring Party which will move up at ZERO - 10.

2. DISPOSITIONS FOR Z plus 1 DAY IN THE EVENT OF A SUCCESSFUL
ASSAULT:-

　　"B" Company plus 4 Lewis Guns "C" Company (not exceeding
100 including Coy Hd.Qrs) Company Headquarters W.21.b.8.7.,
Garrison New Line.

　　"A" Company Old Front Line - immediate counter-attack for
new Front Line.　Company Headquarters W.21.b.60.45.

　　"C" Company (less 4 Lewis Gun Sections) TORRENS SUPPORT.
Replace "A" Company if latter move forward and garrison old
Front Line.　Company Headquarters W.21.a.3.0.

　　"D" Company MELBOURNE TRENCH:- Battalion Reserve.

(1)　The guiding principle of the Defence is:-
　　That the new front line must be held or, if lost,
　　recaptured by immediate counter-attack.
(2)　That there must always be troops available to immediately
　　garrison the old front line.
　　To enable this to be carried into effect it is essential
that the closest liaison must be maintained between Company
Commanders
　　The Signal Station at W.21.b.60.45 will remain in position.
　　Troops will be disposed as above by 2 a.m. 1st July.

　　　　　　　　　　　　　　　　　　　C o n t i n u e d.

Addenda and Amendments to O.O.26 - Continued.

3. Reference 54th Brigade Order No.163, para 38, amend as under:-
   Password "JOHNNY" answer "WALKER". (WALKER)

4. "A" Company Carrying Party will leave their equipment near the Dumps. They will carry Rifles and Bandoliers.

   "C" Company Wiring Parties will leave equipment in TORRENS SUPPORT.

5. Lewis Gun Officer will arrange for two spare Lewis Guns to be at Battalion Headquarters to replace any damaged in action.

29.6.1918.

A.E. Percival Lt.Colonel
Commanding 2nd Bn.Bedfordshire Regiment.

Distribution as per Order No.26.

NIGHT:

Advance Party of 2nd Bn.BEDFORDSHIRE WILTS ORDER BEDFORDSHIRE REGT.
===

(a) **RELAY POSTS:**
    The Stretcher Bearers of "B" and "C" Companies will accompany their Coys.
    and will evacuate as far as the Relay Post of R.A.P.N/2.

(b) Four Relay Squads under Sergt. Pannell will be established
    at G.24.a.7.2.
    These Squads will take over cases from the Company Stretcher Bearers
    and will carry as far as the R.A.P. at G.23.d.8.6.

(c) R.A.P.'s will consist of the R.A.P.
    The Four Bearer Squads mentioned in para (b) will be composed as under:-

    8 men to be detailed by Bty. Field Ambulance.
    4 men to be detailed by "A" Company.
    4 men to be detailed by "B" Company.
    4 men to be detailed by "C" Company.

    "A" and "D" Companies will each detail 3 trained Stretcher Bearers
    and 2 carriers for this work. They will report to the Medical Officer
    at Battalion Headquarters at 10.b.7.4. at 7.0 p.m. on the 15th inst.

    The Relay Post at 24.a.7.2. will remain in position until relieved
    by the Medical Officer when men detailed by "A" and "D" Companies
    will rejoin their Companies.

Signed

2nd Lieut. & Adjt.
2nd Battalion Bedfordshire Regiment.

Issued to all concerned.

SECRET.   2nd Bn. Bedfordshire Regiment.   Order No. 31.

Copy No. ....

Reference Maps:- Sheet 62.d.N.E. and N.W.1/20,000.

1. **INTENTION.**
   The Battalion will relieve the 56th Battalion A.I.F. on the night 30/31st July, 1918, as Battalion in Brigade Reserve.

2. **RELIEF.**
   "A" Coy will relieve "A" Coy & ½ "B" Coy 56th Bn.A.I.F.
   "B" Coy will relieve "D" Coy 56th Bn.A.I.F.
   "C" Coy will relieve "C" Coy and ½ "B" Coy 56th Bn.A.I.F.
   "D" Company will take up their position in RAVINE J.22.c.9.

3. **STARTING POINT AND TIME.**
   Cross Roads at C.29.d.8.8.   TIME:- 8.15 p.m.

4. **ORDER OF MARCH.**
   "B", "A", Headquarters, "C", "D".
   100 yards interval will be maintained between platoons.

5. **ROUTE AND GUIDES.**
   C.29.d.8.8. - C.6.b. - HEILLY - J.13.b.7.6. -
   J.14.a & b - J.15.a & d.
   Guides will be met at J.15 Central.

6. **TRANSPORT.**
   One Limber per Company and Headquarters will carry Lewis Guns, Drums, one dixie per platoon, etc., to J.15.a.Central.

7. **RATION DUMP.**
   Ration Dump will be at J.22.c.45/50.

8. **WATER SUPPLY.**
   One water cart will remain at the Ration Dump and be refilled nightly at HEILLY.
   25 Tins of water for each of "A" "B" and "C" Coys will be sent up nightly.

9. **ADVANCE PARTY.**
   Advance parties will proceed under Company arrangements.
   The Sergeant Cook, 1 N.C.O. and 1 Runner from Battalion Headquarters will report to 2nd Lieut. DAVIES at 5 p.m.

10. **TRENCH STORES.**
    Receipts will be given for Trench Stores, Maps, Fortress Rations, Defence Schemes, etc. taken over and sent to Headquarters by 9 a.m. 31st inst.   Location of Ammunition and Other dumps will be given.

11. **MOVEMENT.**
    Movement by day must be reduced to the minimum. All ranks will keep to the trenches during daylight.

12. **A.A.GUNS**
    Each Company and Bn.Hd.Qrs will man two A.A.Guns, one N.C.O. to be responsible for each pair of guns.

13. **T.M.BATTERY.**
    Will move with Battalion and remain at Bn.Hd.Qrs until positions are decided upon.

14. **COMPLETION OF RELIEF.**
    Will be reported as follows:-
    "A" Coy BLACK, "B" Coy RED.   "C" Coy GREEN.   "D" Coy BLUE.
    Dispositions with sketch map will be sent in by midday 31st.

15. **A C K N O W L E D G E.**

30.7.1918.   Lieutenant
                Asst.Adjutant 2nd Bn. Bedfordshire Regiment.

Distribution on reverse.

OPERATION ORDER NO.31. dated 30.7.17. Distribution.

Copy No.1   C.O.
     2   54th Bde
     3   O.C. "A" Coy
     4   O.C. "B" Coy
     5   O.C. "C" Coy
     6   O.C. "D" Coy
     7   Quartermaster.
     8   Transport Officer.
     9   2nd Lt. DAVIES
    10   R.S.M.
    11   War Diary
    12   War Diary
    13   File
    14   56th Bn.A.I.F.
    15   54th T.M.B.

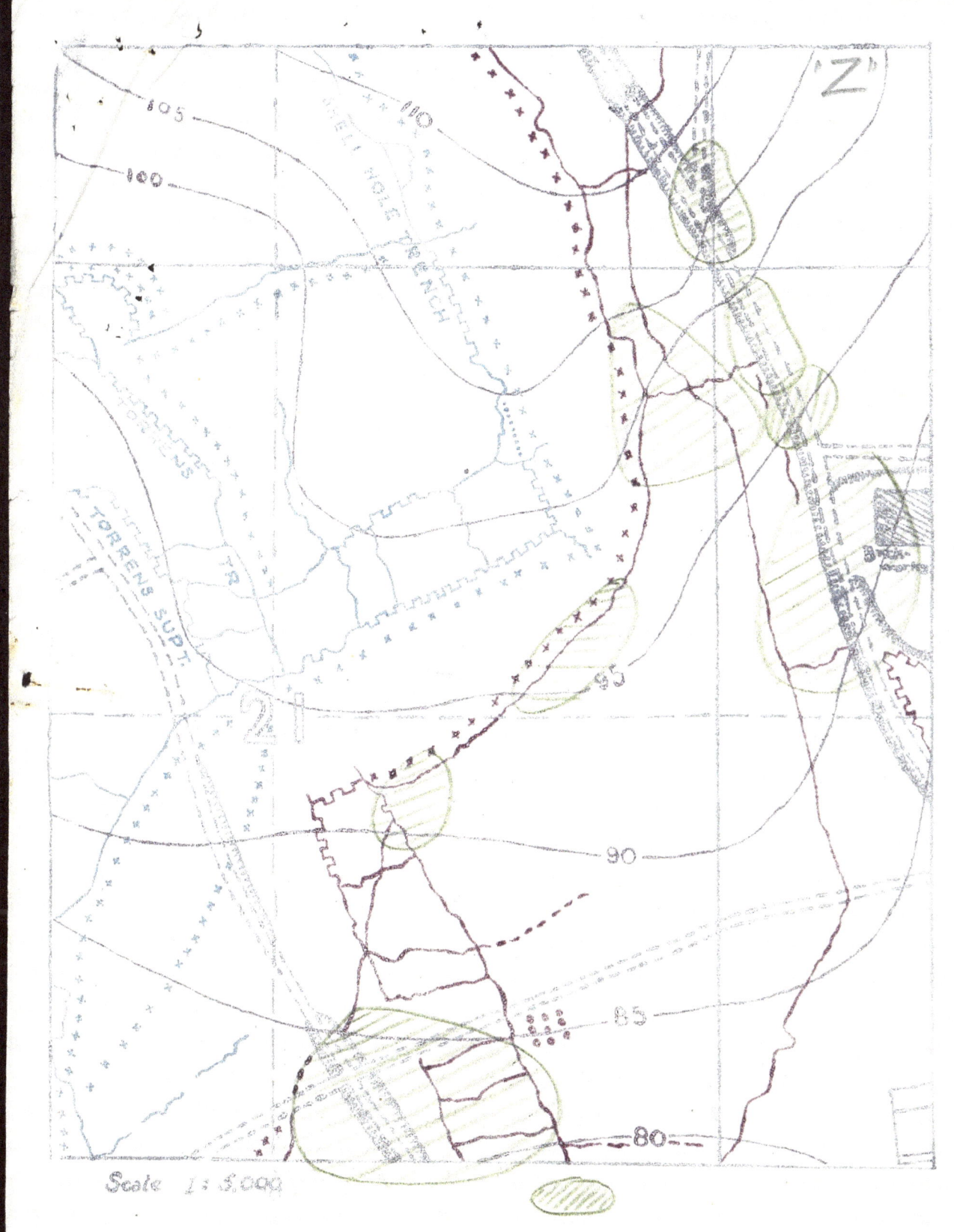

On nights of 22nd/23rd and 27th/28th June.
Gas in Green mixed with smoke.
2 shoots, sometimes 3 shoots, per night, at different times.

"G" Day.

Smoke in black -
Smoke and gas in green -   } Zero minus 10 minutes - Zero.

Secret.

Officer Commanding,
    "B" Company
    "C" Company.
54th Infantry Brigade (for information)

PROBABLE PROGRAMME FOR TRAINING 21st to 30th JUNE.

Friday 21st June.
    Officers and N.C.O's inspect line and practice trenches.
    Spitlock trenches.

Saturday 22nd June.

MORNING.
- "B" Company — Practice Attack with N.C.O's.
- "C" Company — Practice wiring — move wire dump to practice trenches.

AFTERNOON.
- "B" Company — Practice over course with whole Company.
- "C" Company — Musketry — Aiming Blindfold (½ hour).
- ("C" Coy N.C.O's attend "B" Coy's Practice)

Sunday 23rd June.

Morning.   "B" and "C" Company Practice Attack. *10.30 am*

Afternoon. Practice crossing uncut wire.

Monday 24th June.

Morning.   "B" Company:- Correction of previous faults.
            N.C.O's visit line.
            Bombing Practice.

            "C" Company:- Drill and Musketry.

Night.   "B" Company:- Practice attack. *10 pm*
            "C" Company:- Wiring.

Tuesday 25th June.

Morning. Practice attack in conjunction with 6th N'Hants. *11-12 Nu*
                                                    3-4

Afternoon. Disposal of Company Commanders. *4-6 Bad.*

Wednesday 26th June.

Morning. Practice attack in conjunction with 6th N'Hants.

Afternoon. Half Holiday. *Night: Join actual*

Thursday 27th June.

Morning.   "B" Company:- Bombing, Musketry and Bayonet Fighting.
            "C" Company:- ————————do————————
            N.C.O's visit line.

Night.   Practice attack in conjunction with 6th N'Hants.

Continued.

Page 2.

Friday 28th June, 1918.

Morning.   "B" Company:-   Bombing, Musketry, and Bayonet Fighting
            "C" Company:-   -----------------do----------------

NIGHT.   "B" Company N.C.O's visit line and practice forming up on tapes.

            "C" Company:-   Carry wire up to front line.

Saturday 29th June, 1918.

            Disposal of Company Commanders.

Sunday 30th June, 1918.

            Holiday.

                                                        Lt.Colonel
22.6.1918.   Commanding 2nd Bn.Bedfordshire Regiment.

SECRET.

Programme of Training June 23rd - 28th.

Date.	Morning.		Afternoon.	Night.
Sunday, 23rd.	"B" Coy. "D" "	Practice Attack. " "	Range Practice. " " N.C.Os visit the Line.	
Monday, 24th.	"B". "D"	Bombing and Bayonet Fighting. Wiring and Musketry.		Practice Attack. Wiring.
Tuesday, 25th.	"B")) "D")	Practice Attack in conjunction with 2nd Bedfords.	Disposal of Company Commanders. 10.30 p.	
Wednesday, 26th.	"B")) "D")	Practice Attack in conjunction with 2nd Bedfords.		Practice attack in conjunction with 2nd Bedfords.
Thursday, 27th.	"B" "D"	Bombing, Musketry and Bayonet Fighting.		Practice attack in conjunction with 2nd Bedfords.
Friday, 28th.	"B" "D"	Bombing, Musketry, and Bayonet Fighting.		N.C.Os. visit the Line.

22.6.1918.

Capt.& Adjt.
6th Northamptonshire Regiment.

2 Beethoven R1
JS 42
July 8

H. G. 75 min

On His Majesty's Service.

D.A.G.
G.H.Q.
3rd Echelon

WAR DIARY or INTELLIGENCE SUMMARY

Army Form C. 2118.

(Erase heading not required.)

Instructions regarding War Diaries and Intelligence Summaries are contained in F. S. Regs., Part II. and the Staff Manual respectively. Title Pages will be prepared in manuscript.

Place	Date	Hour	Summary of Events and Information	Remarks and references to Appendices
ALBERT.	30-6-18		The Battalion took part in Active Operations N.W. of ALBERT.	I
ALBERT	1-7-18		Battalion in disposition as appendix I. Lieut. A.E.Hammond and 2nd Lieut. H.W.Haward Wounded 30-6-18. 2nd Lieut.G.A.L.Kerr,Missing 2nd Lieut. T.N.Donovan proceeded to England to join R.A.F. on 30-6-18. Casualties O.R.s. ending noon 1st. Killed 8; Wounded 46; Missing 1.	II
ALBERT.	2-7-18		Battalion in disposition as appendix I. Lieut. J.L.Ash Killed 2-7-18. 2nd Lieut. W.Hughes MC. and 2nd Lieut. R.W.Curtice (54th T.M.B.) Wounded 2-7-18 Casualties ending noon 2nd (24 hrs) Killed 10; Wounded 38; Missing 2.	
ALBERT.	3-7-18		The Battalion was relieved in the line by the 7th Bn. The "Queens" Regt and after completion of relief marched to billets in WARLOY.	
WARLOY.	4-7-18		Battalion in billets resting. The Battalion was in Brigade Reserve.	
WARLOY.	5-7-18		Battalion resting in Billets.	
WARLOY.	6-7-18		Battalion resting in Billets. Lieut. F.S.Lapper appointed Assistant Adjutant. 2nd Lieut.A.W.G.Smith appointed Bn.L.G.Offr.	
WARLOY.	7-7-18		Part of the Battalion were engaged in Working Parties. Draft of 87 Other Ranks arrived from the Base. Lieut.Colonel A.E.Percival DSO.MC. proceeded to 54th Inf. Bde to command the Brigade during the absence of the G.O.C. on leave. Major L.H.Keep. MC. took over command of the Battalion.	
WARLOY.	8-7-18		Battalion in billets. In the evening the Battalion practised manning "Battle Positions". 2nd Lieut. A.G.Brown and a draft of 22 Other Ranks arrived from the Base. 2nd Lieut. J.R.Taylor attached to the 54th Trench Mortar Battery.	
WARLOY.	9-7-18		Part of the Battalion were finding Working Parties. A draft of 51 Other Ranks arrived from the Base. Lieut. H.B.Stewart and 2nd Lieut.A.W.G.Smith were evacuated to Hospital Sick.	
WARLOY.	10-7-18		Battalion finding Working Parties. No.9126 Sergt. Cobbold A.F. awarded the Meritorious Service Medal (Supp.L.G. D/10-7-18)	
WARLOY.	11-7-18		Battalion resting in Billets. Lieut. J.M.Glen arrived from the Base. Major J.T.Payne, MC. (General List) attached to the Battalion for one month.	

Continued.

Army Form C. 2118.

WAR DIARY
or
INTELLIGENCE SUMMARY

PAGE 2.

(Erase heading not required.)

Instructions regarding War Diaries and Intelligence Summaries are contained in F.S. Regs., Part II. and the Staff Manual respectively. Title Pages will be prepared in manuscript.

Place	Date	Hour	Summary of Events and Information	Remarks and references to Appendices
	12-7-18		At 5.30 p.m. the Battalion embussed just outside CONTAY and proceeded to FERRIERES arriving at about 10.0 p.m.	III
FERRIERES	13-7-18		Battalion passed into G.H.Q. Reserve and ready to move at 9 hrs notice.	IV
FERRIERES	14-7-18		Battalion resting in billets and re-fitting. Captain R.L.V.Doake and 30 Other Ranks arrived from the Base	
FERRIERES	15-7-18		Battalion resting in billets and re-fitting. Battalion training under O.C. Companies. Lewis Gunners, Scouts etc undergoing instruction under their respective Officers.	V
FERRIERES	16-7-18		2nd Lieut. J.R.Taylor taken on the establishment of the 54th Trench Mortar Battery and struck off strength of the Battalion from 15-7-18. Battalion training at FERRIERES under O.C. Companies.	
FERRIERES	17-7-18		Captain H.Seys-Phillips appointed Acting Adjutant. Battalion training at FERRIERES.	
FERRIERES	18-7-18		A party of 8 Other Ranks proceeded to the 4th Army Rest Camp near EU. Lieut. G.N.Groves R.A.M.C. relieved Capt. J.Thompson as Medical Officer whilst on leave. Battalion training at FERRIERES.	
FERRIERES	19-7-18		Lieut. W.Fielden proceeded to join the Machine Gun School, Grantham on 18-7-18 and struck off strength of the Battalion from that date. Battalion training at FERRIERES under O.C. Companies including Artillery Formation fire and movement.	
FERRIERES	20-7-18		The Battalion paraded at 10 a.m. for Church Parade at GUIGNEMICOURT. At 12 noon the Battalion formed up at practiced the Normal Formation for the Attack.	
FERRIERES	21-7-18		Battalion training at FERRIERES.	
FERRIERES	22-7-18		Battalion training under O.C.Companies. A draft of 12 Other Ranks arrived from the Base Captain G.E.Gott arrived from the Base.	
FERRIERES	23-7-18		Battalion training, during the morning a Bn. Guard Mounting Competition was held. A draft of 10 Other Ranks arrived from the Base.	
FERRIERES	24-7-18b		Battalion training at FERRIERES.	
FERRIERES	25-7-18		Representation parades awards decoration presentation Battalion training. The Corps Commander presented decorations to N.C.O.s and men of the Battalion	V
FERRIERES	26-7-18		Battalion attended the Bde Sports and won 75% of the prizes. Weather awful everybody had a very enjoyable day in spite of the rain.	VI
FERRIERES	27-7-18		The following N.C.O.s and men were awarded the Military Medal. No.33978 Cpl. Clifton H. No.29838 Cpl. Sawkins E. attached to 54th Trench Mortar Battery. and No.30231 Pte. Petty A.V. attached to the 54th Trench Mortar Battery.	

Continued --------

Army Form C. 2118.

WAR DIARY
or
INTELLIGENCE SUMMARY

PAGE 3.

(Erase heading not required.)

Place	Date	Hour	Summary of Events and Information	Remarks and references to Appendices
FERRIERES.	28-7-18		Battalion resting in billets.	
FERRIERES.	29-7-18		At 12 noon the Battalion embussed at QUERRIEU and marched to trenches just outside FRANVILLERS (Ref.map:-Sheet 62E) the Battalion being in Divisional Reserve. 2nd Lieut. A.G.Brown proceeded to join the 1/1st Bn.Hertfordshire Regt and struck off strength of the Battalion from 29th inst. A draft of 6 Other Ranks arrived from the Base.	
FRANVILLERS.	30-7-18		The Battalion in Divisional Reserve in trenches outside FRANVILLERS. In the evening the Battalion proceeded to the line to relieve the 56th Australian Bn. Lieut.Colonel A.E.Percival. DSO.MC. returns from 54th Bde and resumes command of the Battalion.	
Line.	31-7-18		Battalion after relieving the 56th Australian Bn. became the Battalion in Brigade Reserve.	

1-8-18

Lieut.Colonel.
Commanding 2nd Battalion Bedfordshire Regiment.

BATTALION ORDERS.   NO.819.
BY
LIEUT.COLONEL. A.E. PERCIVAL. DSO. MC.
COMMANDING 2ND BATTALION BEDFORDSHIRE REGIMENT.
B.E.F................ 1.7.18.

1. INCREASES. No.16749 Pte.Knight.E.W. "C" Company having rejoined
   the Battalion on 1.7.18. is taken on strength
   accordingly.

2. DECREASES. 2/Lieut.T.N.Donovan having been accepted, on probation,
   for employment with the Royal Air Force is struck off
   strength from 1.7.18.
   Authority:- A.G.2154/275 (O) dt.27.6.18.- R.A.F.934/34/
   68 (A) dt.22.6.18.

3. CASUALTIES. The Commanding Officer regrets to announce the
   following Casualties on 30th June, 1918.

   WOUNDED IN ACTION.   "A" Company.
   49675 Pte.H.Freeman   25841 Pte.A.Hilliard.   49655 Pte.H.J.Henley.
   39758 Pte.J.Stammers

                                "B" Company.
   17956 Pte.E.Albon   25230 Pte.H.Bird   41528 Pte.H.Burn.
   37591 Cpl.E.H.Briston   18023 A/Sgt.O.Crawley   20324 Sgt.W.Deighton
   20284 Pte.M.P.Evans   50195 Pte.G.Eastaway
   18057 L/c.H.Fernyhough   12608 Pte.O.Goldsmith   14580 Pte.G.Hayden
   32128 L/c.G.Houghton   25954 Pte.B.J.Hobbs   15897 Cpl.W.F.Jacklin
   29471 Pte.J.H.Lilley   13293 L/c.R.J.Hinns   14322 Pte.H.Mattin
   29287 Pte.A.G.Pegg   202671 Pte.B.Rolf   48974 Pte.C.W.Raynor
   15782 Cpl.T.J.Squires   10857 Pte.J.W.Platts   41559 Pte.A.S.Smith
   16531 Pte.P.Single   43556 Pte.W.Widswell   18631 Pte.S.Todd
   18531 Pte.W.Woodfield

                                "C" Company.
   6594   Pte.C.Ansell   49308 Pte.J.W.Bennett   40241 L/c.W.T.Davison
   9603   Pte.W.Giles   49233 Pte.E.V.Hancock   14446 Sgt.S.W.Jaggard
   206737 Pte.A.Lauderdale   271706 Pte.H.J.Mann   21607 Pte.G.Price.
   47415 Pte.D.Plews   16575 Pte.A.Pindred   203338 Pte.C.Thurley
   43799 Pte.S.Trewhella

   WOUNDED AND REMAINING AT DUTY.
   41539 Pte.B.Fardon,   "B" Company.
   39837 L/c.H.B.Wadsworth, "D" Company.

4. COURSES.   The undermentioned will hold themselves in readiness to
   proceed on a III Corps Lewis Gun Course assembling on
   3rd July.
      18285 Cpl.Ellis. W.A.   "C" Company.
      266424 Pte.Hilderbrand.F. "C" Company.

5. RATE OF   The rate of Exchange for issue of Cash to the troops
   EXCHANGE. of the Expeditionary Force has been fixed at the rate
              of 5 francs equals 3 shillings and eight pence for
              the month of July 1918.
              (G.R.O. 4385 dt.28.6.18).

                                                    Lieut. for
                              Adjutant, 2nd Bn. Bedfordshire Regiment.

ACCOUNT OF OPERATIONS AT BOUZINCOURT SPUR
30TH JUNE to 3RD JULY, 1918.

At 9.35 p.m. on the 30th June the 2nd Bedfordshire Regiment. in conjunction with the 12th Division on left and 6th Northamptons on right attacked the enemy trenches on the BOUZINCOURT SPUR N.W. of ALBERT. The attack was carried out by "B" Company under Lieut. H.B.Stewart, with "C" Company under Lieut. K.J.Ritchie, responsible for wiring the captured line and one platoon of "A" Company Carrying Party. "A" Company (less one Platoon) and "D" Company were in reserve in MELBOURNE TRENCH.

The attack was carried out under a smoke screen and Stokes Barrages and was entirely successful, all objectives being gained, a large number of the enemy killed, three Machine Guns captured and about 20 prisoners taken.

In addition Lieut. W.S.Oliver-Jones with a small party of men successfully bombed a number of dug-outs in the sunken road which were full of the enemy.

Actual casualties during the assault was about one Officer 35 Other Ranks.

Owing to enemy heavy artillery and Machine Gun fire "C" Company were unable to get any wire out and a Counter Attack made by the enemy at 2.0 a.m. on 1st July succeeded in driving in our most advanced posts.

At 7.30 a.m. a Counter Attack organised by Lieut. H.B.Stewart in conjunction with the 6th Queens on the left succeeded in regaining these posts but they were again lost at 4.30 p.m. after a long bombing contest.

At 8.50 p.m. the enemy delivered a heavy counter attack on the whole front and succeeded in driving in the 12th Division on our left from their advanced position. "B" Company however held fast and at 2.0 a.m on the 2nd July they were relieved by "D" Company under Captain Reiss.MC.MM

A quieter day followed but at 9.25 p.m. after two hours heavy shelling, in the course of which the enemy obliterated a large portion and knocked out two Lewis Gun teams, the enemy attacked under a very heavy 5.9" barrage and succeeded in recapturing their original front line in spite of a magnificent resistance put up by a party under Captain Reiss and Lieut. Hughes.

The total Casualties during the attack were 7 officers and 146 Other Ranks.

The following immediate awards were received for this action:-

Captain P.J.Reiss. MC. MM.   BAR TO MILITARY CROSS.
Lieut. H.B.Stewart.   MILITARY CROSS.
Lieut. W.S.Oliver-Jones.   MILITARY CROSS.
No.10731 Sergt. Clarke R. "B" Company.   D.C.M.
No.17442 Pte. Goodliffe A. MM. "B" Company. D.C.M.

                                                        Major.
                                               for Lt.Colonel
12-8-18   Commanding 2nd Battalion Bedfordshire Regiment.

Secret. ~~War Diary~~ (1)   1/1   O.O.24

All Coys
Sgt Hills.   1-7-18.

1. "D" Coy will relieve "B" Coy & attached troops in the front line on the night of the 1st/2nd inst.

2. On completion of relief "B" Coy will be accommodated in MELBOURNE TR.

3. "D" Coy will hold the line with approx. 90 O.R. including 7 L.G. teams.

4. Lewis Guns will be placed as shewn in attached sketch.

5. "D" Coy L.G. teams will take over positions by 9.0 pm on the 1st inst. As soon as these positions are taken over all troops attached to "B" Coy (except "D" Coys 6 Lewis Gunners) will immediately rejoin their Coys.

6. "D" Coy (less Lewis Gun teams) will relieve "B" Coy as circumstances permit any time after 11.30 pm on the 1st inst. They will carry up rations, tea & water

for the whole Company.

7. Route. CAREY TR. – BOUNDARY TR.

8. Platoon representatives of "D" Coy will proceed in advance in charge of an officer & will meet their platoons at W 15 d 4 0 & guide them to their positions.

9. "B" Coy will hand over all S.O.S. Rockets, Very lights etc to "D" Coy. They will also hand over all filled L.G. Drums now in possession of "B" Coy Gunners & will replenish these from dump at Bn H.Q's.

10. Completion of Relief will be reported by code word 'RICE'.

11. Snipers now attached to "B" Coy will be relieved by 4 Snipers to be attached to "D" Coy under L/Cpl HUTCHINGS.

12. Acknowledge.

A.L. Percival
Lieut Col.

3 p.m

Para 2 (Cont'd)

Bombing blocks will be formed on the left at:-

    W 15d 65
    W 15d 80
    W 15d 90

in case the left coy. do not reach their objectives.

Temporary blocks, until consolidation is finished at:-

    ~~W 22 a 00.75~~
  + W 22 a 05.75
  + W 22 a 05.65

Blocks at (permanent)
    W 21 b 85.75
  + W 21 b 90.70

SECRET.   Copy No......

2ND BN. BEDFORDSHIRE REGT.   ORDER NO. 28.

Reference Map. BEAULIS & AMIENS SHEETS.

1. The Battalion will be relieved by 15th Bn. London Regt.

2. The Battalion will move to FERRIERES tomorrow by bus. Time and embussing point will be notified later.

3. The Battalion will move out in Fighting Order. Blankets will be carried rolled over the Haversack. One Lewis Gun and 20 Drums per Platoon will be taken.

4. Movement to the embussing point will be by Platoons at 100 yards distance.

5. Embussing Strengths will be rendered to Orderly Room by 10 p.m. tonight.

6. One N.C.O per Company and Headquarters will report to the Assistant Adjutant, when required in order to allot buses at the embussing point.

7. Guides on the scale of 1 per Platoon and 2 for Battalion H.Q. will meet the 15th Londons at their debussing point. Place and time to be notified later.

8. The Transport will move by road leaving about 4.0 a.m.

9. Sufficient cooking utensils for 12th inst will be retained and taken on the baggage lorry. This lorry will also take Officer's Valises, one Mess Box per Company and the remaining Orderly Room boxes.

10. All Tents and shelters will be handed over to the 15th Londons, and receipts obtained and sent to Orderly Room by 10 p.m. 12th inst. All tents and shelters in the new area will be taken over and receipts given for them, a copy being sent to Battalion H.Q. by 10 p.m. the 12th inst.

11. All Defence Schemes and accompanying Maps and documents relating to the sector, S.O.S. Rockets etc. will be handed over to the incoming Unit, receipts obtained and forwarded as in para.10.

12. ACKNOWLEDGE.

                                                  CAPTAIN & A/ADJUTANT
11.7.18.
                                   2ND BN. BEDFORDSHIRE REGIMENT.

         Copies to:-   No.1. Commanding Officer.
                           2. 54th Bde.
                           3   O.C. "A" Company.
                           4. O.C. "B" Company.
                           5. O.C. "C" Company.
                           6. O.C. "D" Company.
                           7. Quartermaster.
                           8. Transport Officer.
                           9. Signalling Officer.
                          10. R.S.M.
                          11. War Diary.
                          12. -do-
                          13. File.
                          14. 15th Bn. London Regt.

All Battalions.
Brigade Training Camp.
Brigade Major.
Brigade Transport Officer.
Brigade Signal Officer.
152 Coy., A.S.C. (for information).

S.C.29.

1. First Line Transport and baggage wagons will move to new area to-morrow morning.

2. Order of march :-
        Brigade Headquarters.
        11th Royal Fusiliers.
        2nd Bedfordshire Regt.
        6th Northamptonshire Regt.
Starting point - Corner of Wood U.28.d.7.5.
Head of column to pass starting point at 4 a.m., moving West.
Usual intervals between vehicles.

3. Column will report to O.C. 152 Coy. A.S.C. at cross roads East of MOLLIENS at B.8.b.6.8. and will come under his orders for rest of march.

4. Transport at present at Brigade Training Camp, under an N.C.O. detailed by O.C., Training Camp, will report to O.C., 152 Coy., A.S.C. at B.8.b.6.8. by 6.30 a.m.

5. Lewis guns and drums required in case the Brigade has to go up into action to-morrow morning will not be carried on transport but will be taken in buses by L.G. teams.

6. Dixies required for to-morrow's dinners will also be taken on buses.

7. Lorries for kit will report as follows, at U.30.c.6.6. at 11 a.m. to-morrow -

        1 for Brigade H.Qrs.
        1 per Battalion.
        1 for Brigade Training Camp.
        1 for Pierrots and Cinema.
All concerned will have guides there to take over.

8. 11th Royal Fusiliers will detail 1 N.C.O., each Battalion and Brigade H.Qrs. 1 O.R., to stay behind and clean up lines. All manure to be buried, and sites of bivouacs left scrupulously clean. After completion they will embus with their battalions.

9. Transport Officers will ensure that all ranks are conversant with Fourth Army M.O. 2039 of 15th May 1918, March Discipline and Traffic Control, for the march.

10. No unauthorised vehicles will accompany transport. Units will make their own arrangements for these.

                      Captain.
                      A/Staff Captain.
                      54th Inf. Brigade.

11th July 1918.

BATTALION ORDERS.   No. 831
BY
MAJOR. L. H. KEEP. MC.
COMMANDING 2ND BN. BEDFORDSHIRE REGIMENT.
B.E.F. .... 14.7.18.

1. **DETAIL.**
   Battalion Orderly Officer:- 2/Lieut.S.E.Dancer. "C" Coy
   Next for Duty:- Lieut.A.F.Woodford. "C" Coy
   Company for Duty:- "A" Company.
   Reveille:- 6.45 a.m.
   Breakfast:- 7.45 a.m.
   Orderly Room:- 2.0 p.m.

2. **TRAINING.** (i) 7.0 a.m. Running Parade under Coy. Orderly Officers.
   Dress:- Shirt sleeves, no puttees.

   9.0 a.m.) Close Order Drill under O.C. Companies on
   to   ) Company Parade Grounds.
   10.30 am) Drums will report to O.C."A" Company.
   Dress:- Musketry Order.

   10.30 am) Specialist training.
   to   )
   12.45 pm)

   Bathing. Companies will march down to bathe in the River at AILLY. Times as under:-
   "A" & "B" Coys -   2.0 p.m.
   "C", "D" Coys & H.Q. 2.30 p.m.

   (ii)(a) Lewis Gun Training. The following will be employed as Instructors; and neither they nor those under instruction will be taken for Guards or other duties or fatigues while the course lasts:-
   Sgt.Turville, H.Qrs.   Q.M.S. Ingall. H.Qrs.

   "A" Company
   Sergt. Baker.   L/Cpl.Adams. T.   L/Cpl. Smith. F.
   Corpl. Dines. S.   Corpl. Fynn. D.   Pte.   Cook. L.P.

   "B" Company
   Sergt.Stone.A.   L/Cpl.Drage.L.   Cpl.Southerden.E.
   L/Cpl.Wykes. A   L/Cpl.Hubbard.   L/Cpl.Britton.
   Corpl.Stokes.

   "C" Company.
   Sergt.King.   L/Cpl.Langford.   Corpl.Carter.

   "D" Company.
   Sgt. Cousins.   Cpl.Coles.

   Classes. (a) Forty eight men partially trained at MOLLIENS AU BOIS last week, for completion of 6 days course.
   (b) 22 men per Company untrained men to undergo the 6 days course.
   Parade behind CHATEAU at 11.0 a.m.

   (iii) Young N.C.Os Class. Parade behind CHATEAU at 11.0 a.m.
   Dress:- Musketry Order.
   Major J.T. Payne will take this Class.

   (iv) Scouts. Parade behind CHATEAU AT 11.0 a.m.
   Dress:- Musketry Order.   Lieut.Tupper will take this Class.

   (v) Remainder will be trained in Musketry, Rifle bombing etc under Company Commanders

3. **INCREASE.**
   No.9068 Sgt.Newham.W.L. "D" Company having rejoined the Battalion on 14.7.18 is taken on strength accordingly.

   No.49006 Pte.Freeman.C.T.having joined the Battalion on 14.7.18 is taken on strength and posted to "C" Company.

   contd.

PUNISHMENT.	No. 8736 Pte. Challis. E. "D" Company was this day awarded 14 days F.P. No.1. for "When on Active Service" Insolence to his superior Officer 13.7.18.
5. EMPLOY.	No. 8736 Pte. Challis. E. "D" Company is returned to duty on completion of sentence.

[signature]

CAPTAIN.

A/ADJUTANT, 2ND BN. BEDFORDSHIRE REGT.

N O T I C E S

Open Air Concert behind the CHATEAU at 5.30 p.m.
Admission free.

Cinema Show in the CINEMA HALL at 7.0 p.m.
Admission 3d.

PLAN OF CENTENNIAL PARADE

LEGEND
Red = 11th R Fus
Brown = 2nd Beds
Green = 6th Northants
Blue = 34th Fd Amb
▣ = Massed Bands
░░░ = Recipients
▣ = Bde HQ

SCALE 1:8000

Beds

SECRET   2ND BN. BEDFORDSHIRE REGT.   ORDER NO.29.

Copy No...
IV

16th July 1918

1. The Division is now in G.H.Q. Reserve at 9 hours notice.

2. The Battalion will be in readiness to move by train or bus. Entraining and embussing points will be as follows:-
   (a) Entraining Stations.
       HANGEST   ...   ...   If moving North.
       SALEUX PROUZEL...   ...   If moving South.

   (b) Embussing point.
       BRIQUESESNIL - FERRIERES ROAD. Head of Column facing E. at W. end of FERRIERES.

3. On receipt of the order "Prepare to Move" Companies will "STAND TO" in billets. The Transport will be packed and all arrangements made ready to move.

4. If moving North the order of March to the entraining Station will be: 6th Northamptonshire Regt., 2nd Bedfordshire Regt., 11th R.Fusiliers.
   If moving South:-
   11th Royal Fusiliers., 2nd Bedford Regt., 6th Northamptonshire Regt.
   Order of embussing:-
   2nd Bedfordshire Regt., 6th Northamptonshire Regt., 11th R.Fusiliers.
   Two N.C.Os per Coy., Transport and Hd.Qrs. will report to Battalion Hd.Qrs. fully equipped with the strength of their Coys, as soon as possible after the warning Order has been received. One of these will proceed on the Advanced Billeting party under Lieut.G.B.Reed - the other will assist in entraining or embussing under Lieut.F.S. Lapper.

5. Until more Lewis Gunners are trained only 6 Lewis Guns per Coy. will be taken and manned. 24 Drums per Gun will be carried.

6. Officer's Valises will be dumped at each Coy.H.Qrs as soon as possible after the warning is received, and will be collected by the Transport Officer.

7. Rations will be issued as per para.13. & waterbottles filled immediately the Warning Order is received. Blankets will be carried on the man.
   Company Commanders will report at Bn.H.Qrs. for instructions as soon as these orders have been complied with & their Coys. are ready to move.

8. Departure of trains   -   Numbers and times.
   (1) If moving South.   From SALEUX.
       No.8.Train (Battn.less "D" Coy &)   ZERO + 6 hours.
                   (1 Cooker & team   )

       No.14 Train("D" Coy. & 1 Cooker & team)   ZERO plus 12 hours.

   (2) If moving North.   From HANGEST-SUR-SOMME.
   Train Nos. complements & times as in (1)
   The advance billeting Party will proceed by No.2 Train. In either case leaving at ZERO hour.

9. Busses. Busses Nos. 9 to 41 inclusive are allotted to the Battn. (including "D" Coy) and will be sub-allotted to Coys. according to strengths on the day

10. In the case of entraining, personnel will arrive at the entraining Station 1 hour and transport 3 hours before time of departure of trains.

11. (a) Horses will be watered before entrainment.
    (b) Units must provide head ropes for tying up horses in the trucks.
    (c) Horses will **not** be unharnessed unless the scheduled time for the journey exceeds 15 hours; 2 men will travel in each truck.

12. Supply and Baggage wagons will entrain with Battalion Baggage wagons, and will report on the order to move being received.

                                                                                 contd.

2nd Bedfords Order No. 29 (contd).

13. Rations.
    (1) Move by rail. The Battalion will entrain with the unexpended portion of the day's rations on the man. Rations for the following day will be carried on the Supply Wagons.
    (2) Move by bus. The Battalion will embus with the unexpended portion of the day's rations and the following day's rations on the man.
    Transport Rations and forage will be carried on 1st Line Transport and Supply Wagons.
    Rations for the 2nd day after embussing or entraining will be delivered to the Battalion by Train transport.

14. Water Carts will travel full.

15. The Signalling Officer will detail 2 cyclist orderlies to report to the Staff Captain or his Representative at the entraining Station 3 hours before the departure of the Battalion's train.

16. The Signallers undergoing training at Brigade Headquarters will join the Battalion for entrainment or embussing.
    The Trench Mortar Section will proceed with the Battery, in No. 2 Train, leaving at ZERO hour.

17. ACKNOWLEDGE.

                                                                         CAPTAIN & A/ADJUTANT.

                               2ND BATTALION BEDFORDSHIRE REGIMENT.

Copies to:-
No.1. Commanding Officer.
No.2. 54th Infantry Bde.
No.3. O.C."A" Coy.
No.4. O.C."B" Coy.
No.5. O.C."C" Coy.
No.6. O.C."D" Coy.
No.7. Quartermaster.
No.8. Transport Officer.
No.9. Signalling Officer.
No.10. Lewis Gun Officer.
No.11. R.S.M.
No.12. Lieut. F.S. Lapper.
No.13. War Diary.
No.14. -do-
No.15. File.

54th Infantry Brigade

Agenda for Conference - 20th July 1918.

1. **Notes on previous week's training.**

    Organisation of L.G. Section.

    Understudies for Section Commanders.

    Coy. Conference before and after parade.

    Compliments to Officers on parade.

    Saluting of young Officers.

    Fitting and cleaning of equipment.

    Lanyards.

2. **Lewis Gun Training.**

    Results of MOLLIENS Course.

    Number of hours worked up to date in new course.

    Training of Instructors in order to reduce size of classes.

    Number of guns in possession.

    Tactical handling of L.G. Section.

3. **Snipers and Scouts.**

    Progress made.

    Duration of course.

    Test about 29th inst.

4. **Next week's work.**

    Ceremonial.

    Drill by Section Commander.

    Lewis Gun Training.

    Musketry (snap shooting and fire control)

    Manoeuvre exercises bringing in handling of double L.G. Section.

    Consolidation - demonstration of how to make blocks.

    Use of Snipers during and after consolidation.

    Tactical exercise for Officers and N.C.Os in afternoon or at night.

    Night work for Scouts and snipers.

5. **Employment of Brigade Instructors.**

   Formation of young N.C.Os School at Brigade Headquarters.

6. **Stokes Gun.**

   Officers and N.C.Os to attend tactical exercises held by Battalions.
   Battalion Commanders to notify Captain Payton when these are being held.

7. **General.**

   Team of 3 Officers for Divisional Race Meeting, etc.

   Instructors from Corps School.

54th Infantry Brigade Sports Meeting.

The Meeting will take place Saturday the 27th July 1918, at J.35.d.3.8. (62.E).

PROGRAMME OF EVENTS.

1. Heats of 100 yards ... ... 11.0 a.m.
   Three entries per unit.

2. Tug of War Heats ... ... 11.15 a.m.
   Best of three pulls; teams of 8, one team per unit.

3. Chariot Race - 75 yards ... ... 12 noon.
   Teams of six. Two men in front, holding hands; three men behind linked up as for a scrum. Outside men of rear rank hold the outside hands of the two men in front. One man stands on the shoulders of the three men and has reins attached to the two leaders. Feet must be kept on shoulders - if driver falls off, chariot must stop until he gets back, otherwise the team is disqualified. Entries 2 teams per unit.
   1st prize .... 30 fr.

4. Boat Race - 100 yards ... ... 12.15 p.m.
   Teams of six and cox. One team per Unit.
   1st prize .... 35 fr.

Lunch Interval.

---

5. Sack Race - 50 yards ... ... 2.0 p.m.
   4 entries per unit.
   Prizes - 1st.. 10 fr., 2nd.. 5 fr.

6. 100 yards Final ... ... 2.15 p.m.
   Prizes - 1st 30 fr., 2nd 20 fr., 3rd 10 fr.

7. Officers' Tug of War - Heats ... ... 2.30 p.m.
   Open to units of the Allied Armies.
   Teams of 8. Best of three pulls. One team per unit.

8. Cross Country Race ... ... 3.0 p.m.
   Open to Units of the Division. Distance about 2 miles. Teams of 8, every man to count.
   1st prize 80 fr. for the winning team. Lieut. Colonel A.E. Percival, D.S.O., M.C. will present a prize of 100 fr. to the first man home, and a prize of 50 fr. for the second man home will be presented by Captain L. W. Diggle.

9. Cooks' Potato Race. ... ... 3.0 p.m.
   Unlimited entries for Units of the Brigade.
   Prizes - 1st 20 fr., 2nd. 10fr., 3rd 5 fr.

0. Officers' Musical Chairs on Mules. ... ... 3.30 p.m.
   Open to Officers of the Allied Armies.

-1-   P.T.O.

11. V.C. Race. ... ... 3.45 p.m.
    Competitors put on Box Respirators, run
    30 yards, pick up wounded man, and run
    home. Two teams per unit.
    Prizes - 1st 20 fr., 2nd 10 fr. per team.

12. Comic Turn-out Competition and Race.
    Judging Costumes ... ... 3.45 p.m.
    Race ... ... 4.0 p.m.
    Open to the Division. Entries unlimited.
    Prizes for turn-out - 1st 20 fr., 2nd 10 fr.
    Prizes for the Race - 1st 20 fr., 2nd 10 fr.

13. Officers' Tug of War Final ... ... 4.15 p.m.

14. Mule Race. ... ... 4.30 p.m.
    For Transport Men. Bare back, no whips or
    spurs; distance 3 furlongs. Three entries
    per unit.
    Prizes - 1st 20 fr., 2nd 10 fr., 3rd 5 fr.

15. Officers' Relay Race ... ... 4.45 p.m.
    Teams of six. Distances will be covered
    as under :-
    a) Running (b) Three-legged (c) Bicycle
    d) Mule (e) Sack.
    One team per unit.

16. Band Race - Handicap. 100 yards. ... ... 5.0 p.m.
    Unlimited entries for Units of the Brigade.
    Prizes - 1st 20 fr., 2nd 10 fr., 3rd 5fr.

17. Relay Race ... ... 5.15 p.m.
    Teams of six, each man to run 200 yards.
    Entries, 1 team per unit. Open to all
    Units of the Allied Armies.
    1st prize 60 fr. for the winning team.

18. Musical Chairs on Mules ... ... 5.30 p.m.
    For Transport Men mounted on mules bare back.
    4 entries per unit.
    Prizes - 1st. 20 fr., 2nd 10 fr., 3rd 5fr.

19. Tug of War Final. ... ... 6.0 p.m.
    1st prize 80 fr. Presented by Lieut. Colonel J.H. Foster.

Distribution of Prizes.

There will be 5 fr. entrance fee for all Officers' events; this money to go towards a sweepstake.

The following units are invited to send in entries :-
11th Royal Fusiliers.   2nd Bedfordshire Regt.   6th Northamptonshire Regt.
54th Inf. Brigade H.Q.   54th T.M. Battery.   152 Company, A.S.C.
                           54th Field Ambulance.

Units to send entries to O.C., 6th Northamptonshire Regt. by midnight, 24th July.

Entries to be sent in by teams - names for individual events.
Nos. 9, 11 and 16 are post entries.

SECRET   2ND BN. BEDFORDSHIRE REGT. PROVISIONAL ORDER NO.30.   Copy No... 12

Reference Map. SHEET 62 E. 1/40,000.   28th July 1918.

---

1. The 54th Infantry Brigade will relieve the 15th Australian Brigade in Divisional Reserve in the FRANVILLERS - LA HOUSSOYE AREA on the 29th July 1918.
   The Battalion will parade in full Marching Order with blankets at 11.30 a.m. and will embus on the FERRIERES - BRIQUEMESNIL ROAD (Q.7.c.) about Noon.
   Embussing strengths will be rendered to Orderly Room by 6.0 p.m. tonight.

2. <u>Lewis Guns</u>. Six Lewis Guns and 20 Drums per Gun will be carried by each Company.
   Rifle Grenade Discharger Cups will be carried by the Transport.

3. <u>Transport</u>. The Transport will leave by road early on the 29th inst. and will be ready to move off tonight.

4. <u>Baggage</u>. Orderly Room Boxes, Mess Boxes, Workshops and all surplus kit will be dumped outside Battalion and Company Hd.Qrs. ready for collection by 8.30 p.m. tonight.
   <u>Officers Valises</u>. Pending allotment of a lorry to the Battalion, Officers Valises will be collected at 8.30 p.m. tonight, if a lorry is available they will be dumped ready for collection by 9.0 a.m. 29th inst.

5. <u>Advance Party</u>. Reconnoitring and Advance Party already detailed will proceed by bus leaving Battalion H.Q. at 8.15 a.m. 29th inst.

6. <u>Rations</u>. Pending further Orders a hot meal will be prepared on the road ready for the Battalion on arrival. Should the final orders not allow of the transport arriving before the Battalion, rations will be issued to the men and camp kettles taken on the busses for hot tea on arrival.

7. The Signallers and Trench Mortar Battery at present attached to Brigade will rejoin the Battalion today and proceed with Battalion Headquarters. The R.E. Platoon will move with the Battalion and join the 80th Field Company, R.E. in the new Area.

8. <u>Battle Surplus</u>. A Details Camp will be arranged in the new Area. Companies will send in a nominal roll of their Battle Surplus to reach Orderly Room by 4.0 p.m. today.

9. <u>Stores</u>. All practice S.A.A., bombs etc. will be handed over to the incoming Unit and receipts obtained and forwarded to Orderly Room.

10. <u>ACKNOWLEDGE</u>.

                                                  Lieutenant.
                        Asst/ Adjutant, 2nd Bn. Bedfordshire Regt.

Copies to:-
- No.1. Commanding Officer.
- No.2. 54th Brigade.
- No.3. Adjutant.
- No.4. O.C. "A" Company.
- No.5. O.C. "B" Company.
- No.6. O.C. "C" Company.
- No.7. O.C. "D" Company.
- No.8. Quartermaster.
- No.9. Transport Officer.
- No.10. R.S.M.
- No.11 & 12. War Diary.
- No.13. File.

Subject:- Divisional Sports.   18th Div. No. 32/4 "Q".

Camp Commandant.	18th M.G.Battn.
18th Div. Art.	8th R.Sussex Pnrs.
18th Div. R.E.	18th Div. Train.
18th Div. Sig. Coy.	No. 18 M.T.Coy.
53rd Inf. Bde.	R.A.M.C.
54th Inf. Bde.	30th M.V.Section.
55th Inf. Bde.	"G". (For information).

Reference my No. as above of 14/7/1918, para. 3 :-

1. The Programme for the Aquatic Sports is as under :-

   (a) 50 yards race open to Other Ranks of 18th Division.

   (b) 100 yards   :   :   :   :   :   :   :   :

   (c) 50 yards race open to Officers of 18th Division.

   (d) Team Race, 6 relays, each of 50 yards.
       Open to Officers and Other Ranks of 18th Division.
       Teams may be entered by :-

          53rd Brigade Group.
          54th   do.
          55th   do.

          R.A. Group.
          Divnl. Troops Group.

   (e) Diving Competition, consisting of :-

          (i) Running dive from spring board.
          (ii) Standing dive from bank approximately 3 feet above water level
          (iii) Standing dive from bank approximately 8 feet above water level

       Open to Other Ranks of 18th Division.

   (f) Water Polo - Teams of 7.
       Open to Officers and Other Ranks of 18th Division.
       Teams may be entered as in (d).
       If all five teams enter, one match will be played off on an earlier date.
       Rules for Water Polo will be circulated later

   (g) Costume Craft Race. - Distance 100 yards.
       Crews may race in any type of craft built by themselves, any number forming the crew, and in any costume.
       One prize will be given to the winners of the race and another prize to the most ingeniously turned out craft and crew.

   (h) R.E. Pontoon Race, 440 yards.
       Open to one team from each Field Company, R.E., conditions to be laid down by C.R.E.

   (i) Greasy Pole.
       Open to all ranks of 18th Division.

2.   For events (a), (b), (c), (e) and (g) one entry may be made by each of the following :-

P.T.O.,

(para. 2 continued).

Inf. Brigade H.Q., T.M. Batteries and Bde. Sig. Sect.	1
Battalions	1 each.
R.A. Headquarters, T.M.Bs. and Sig. Section.	1
R.A. Brigades.	1 each.
D.A.C.	1
R.E.	1
R.A.M.C.	1
Div. Train (to include M.V.S.) ..	1
M.T. Company.	1
Divnl. H.Q. (to include No. 1 Sect. Sig. Coy.)	1

The same man may only be entered for one of the three individual events, (a), (b) and (e).

3. The aquatic sports will be held at PICQUIGNY on 28th July.
    Entries to reach this office by 25th July.
    Rank, name and unit to be stated for events (a), (b), (c) and (e).
    Name of groups or units only required for events (d), (f), (g) & (h).

4. List of prizes will be circulated later.

5. Aquatic representative from each Brigade, R.A., R.E., and R.A.M.C. will meet D.A.A.G. at Headquarters, 53rd Infantry Brigade, PICQUIGNY, at 2 p.m. 17th instant, to view site for the sports.

6. A rough sketch of the site will be circulated later, when details have been fixed.

16th July, 1918.

Lieut. Colonel,
A.A. & Q.M.G. 18th Division.

18th Div. No. 32/4 "Q"

Subject:- Sports.

....

1.   As a result of a representative meeting held at D.H.Q. on 15th July, it was decided that the following events would be held under Divisional, Brigade, or Unit arrangements:-

July 20th.	Boxing Tournament.	55th Brigade.
" 21st.	do.	53rd "
" 22nd.	Sports and Aquatic Meeting.	R. Sussex Pnrs.
" 24th.	do.	Royal Engrs.
" 25th.	Divl. Race Meeting.	
" 25th.	Divl. (3rd) Anniversary Dinner.	
" 27th.	Sports.	54th Brigade.
" 28th.	Divl. Aquatic Sports.	
" 29th.	Divl. Boxing Tournament.	

2.   The following events will also be held, but dates have not yet been fixed:-

        Boxing Tournament.)
        Horse Show.   ) R.A.
        Sports. ... ... Div. Train.
        Old English Games. D.H.Q.

3.   The following dates are available, and it is hoped that as far as possible the

        R.A. Horse Show,
        Div. Train Sports and
        D.H.Q. Old English Games

may be arranged for these dates:- July 23rd, 26th and 30th.

4.   As regards boxing, all elementary bouts must take place, and entries sent for Divl. Tournament before July 26th.

5.   As regards the various Sports, etc., it was decided at the Meeting that there should be at least one open event at each fixture, Boxing excepted.

6.   It is particularly requested that a copy of these events be published in a prominent position in every Camp and Billet, and that men be encouraged to attend each meeting so far as the Training Programme will admit.

7.   Units will inform D.H.Q. of the exact location of each event, and also the description of "open events" as early as possible. This information will in turn be published in D.R.Os.

Lieut.-Colonel,
A.A. & Q.M.G., 18th Division.

17th July, 1918.

Distribution - All Units.
      "G".

BOXING COMPETITION

WELTER WEIGHTS

	1st round	2nd round.	Semi-final
1.	Sgt.Lovell. "C" Coy. 9-7. Bye	1. 2 v 8	
2.	L/Cpl.Allen.10.3. v Pte.Hammill.P. "B" Coy.10-4.	2. 3 v 5	
3.	Pte.Plumb. "C" Coy.9-4. Bye.	3. 4 v 1	1. 1 v 4
4.	L/C.Penn 10-3 v Drm.Ross. 9-10. "D" Coy	4. 6 v 7	
5.	Drm.Skipper 10-2 v L/Cpl.Hawkins.A. "B" Coy.10 st.		2. 2 v 3
6.	Pte.Spiller. "C" Coy 10-3 Bye.		
7.	Pte.H.Porter. "B" Coy 10-1 Bye.		
8.	Pte.G.Jeffs. 9-13. Bye.		

1st prize to the value of 40 francs.
2nd   "   "   "   "   " 30   "
3rd   "   "   "   "   " 20   "

Best loser. There will also be a prize to the value of 20 francs for the best loser from for the whole competition.

16.7.18.

Asst. Adjutant, 2nd Bn. Bedfordshire Regiment.   Lieutenant.

BOXING KOMPETITION

The Battalion Boxing Competition will be held at the WHITE CHATEAU on Thursday the 18th inst. at 5.0 p.m.
Contests will be 3 rounds of 2 minutes, under R.N. and A.B.A.Rules.

      JUDGES:-   Captain. Doake. MC.
                    Major.J.T.Payne. D.C.M.

      REFEREE:-   R.S.M. Armstrong.

      M.C. :-   Sergeant. G. Smith.

      TIMEKEEPER:-   Lieut. Glen.

The Medical Officer will be in attendance and will test competitors before entering the ring.

HEAVY-WEIGHT :-

1. Pte.Suffolk.W.A. "B" Coy. 11-8 Bye
2. Pte.Coasby. "D" Coy. 11-7 Bye
3. Dr. Jones. 11.12.Bye
4. ~~Sgt Pearce~~ V ~~Sgt. Blake~~
   "A" Coy.11-6   "A" Coy 11-7

        1st prize to value 25 francs.
        2nd   : : :: 15 :

MIDDLE-WEIGHT.

    ~~Sgt.Coxall.10-10 V Pte.Hebbington.11st~~

    Pte.Dickens.F.   V Pte.Prentice.11st
    "B" Coy.11-2.   "A" Coy.

        1st prize to value of 20 francs
        2nd : : : :10 :

SPECIAL CONTEST. 6 rounds of 2 minutes.

    ~~Pte.Smith.E.~~   V ~~Pte. Jones. "D" Coy~~
    "A" Coy. 10-3.   9-7

        Prize to value of 25 francs.

WELTER WEIGHT. P.T.O.

The Competition will be continued on Friday evening at 5.30 p.m. if unfinished on Thursday.

16.7.18.

                                  Lieutenant.
        Asst.Adjutant, 2nd Bn. Bedfordshire Regiment.

54th Inf. Bde.

18th Division

2nd BATTALION

BEDFORDSHIRE REGIMENT

AUGUST 1918

Army Form C. 2118.

WAR DIARY
or
INTELLIGENCE SUMMARY.
(Erase heading not required.)

Instructions regarding War Diaries and Intelligence Summaries are contained in F.S. Regs., Part II. and the Staff Manual respectively. Title pages will be prepared in manuscript.

Place	Date	Hour	Summary of Events and Information	Remarks and references to Appendices
In Field.	1st August 1918		Battalion in Brigade Reserve.- dispositions as on 31st July. 39 O.R's (chiefly W.O's & N.C.Os) arrived from 7th Bedfordshire Regt.Training Cadre.	
	2nd August.		Battalion relieved "A" & "B" Coys 11th Royal Fusiliers & "A" & "B" Coys.6th Northamptons in Line BRAY-CORBIE ROAD to SOMME (Ref. Map. Sheet 62.d. N.E. 2/20,000. Casualties - 4 O.R. Wounded.	
	3rd August.		Battalion in dispositions as for 2nd inst. Casualties:- 3 O.R. Killed., 1 O.R. wounded.	
	4th August.		Battalion in dispositions as for 2nd inst. Casualties - 2 O.R.Wounded. Capt.S.E.D.Cline., Lieut.H.de Buriatte., 2/Lieut.T.H.Flavell., 2/Lieut.A.D.Greenwood and 2nd Lieut. J. Kerr, joined Battalion from 7th Bedfordshire Regt. Training Cadre. Major.J.T.Payne MC.(General List) proceeded to command No.2. R.T.C. Lieut.(A/Capt) P.J.Reiss. MC. MM. awarded bar to M.C. Lieut.H.B.Stewart and Lieut.W.S.Oliver-Jones awarded Military Cross. No.10731 Sgt.Clarke. C. & No. 17442 Pte A.Goodliffe.MM. awarded D.C.M.	
	5th August.		Battalion relieved by 10th London Regt. On being relieved Battalion took over frontage of 8th East Surrey Regt(55th Bde). Dispositions as follows:- "C" Coy. from K.20.c.4.8. to BRAY - CORBIE ROAD exclusive, at K.20.a.2.9. "D" Coy. from K.25.b.6.6. to BRAY - CORBIE ROAD.c.4.8. "A" Coy. COOLGARDIE TRENCH from J.24.c.3.4. to BRAY - CORBIE ROAD. "B" Coy. from J.24.d.8.5. to BRAY - CORBIE ROAD K.19.a.20.99. (Ref. Map. Sheet.62.D. N.E.) Casualties:- 2/Lieut.P.A.Page. MC. Wounded., 1 O.R. Wounded.	
	6th August		Bosche attacked our Line & penetrated into several positions (see report) MARKED X Major. L.H. Keep. MC in command of Battalion in the line. Casualties:- Lieut.E.S.Lapper-Smith } 2/Lieut.C.King-Smith } Wounded Killed in Action, 6 O.R. 2/Lieut.W.G.Mc.Jannet} Wounded. 38 O.R. Lieut.D.D.Warren, } Missing. Missing. 71 O.R. Lieut.A.F.Woodford }	

Army Form C. 2118.

WAR DIARY
or
INTELLIGENCE SUMMARY.

(Erase heading not required.)

Instructions regarding War Diaries and Intelligence Summaries are contained in F. S. Regs., Part II and the Staff Manual respectively. Title pages will be prepared in manuscript.

Place	Date	Hour	Summary of Events and Information	Remarks and references to Appendices
In Field.	7th August		Battalion relieved by 8th London Regt and became Battalion in Brigade Reserve in attack by Fusiliers & Northamptons to recover original British Front Line from K.14.a.4.0 to K.25.b.7.8. Casualties:- Lieut. K.J.Ritchie. Wounded. Killed in Action - 4 O.R. Lieut. S.G.Hague.MC.Wounded still at duty. Wounded - 21 O.R. Missing - 1 O.R.	
	8th August		Battalion relieved by Sussex Regt (12th Division) and accomodated in Bank near BONNAY. Casualties:- 3 O.R. Wounded.	
	9th August		Battalion moved to BALLARAT - ROMA LINE and vicinity of same between BRAY - CORBIE ROAD and J.10.b.8.0. Battalion on Right as far north as J.17.a.2.7. (Ref.Map. Sheet.62.D. N.E.)	
	10th August		On night 10th/11th inst Battalion relieved 20th London Regt. as Battalion in Brigade Reserve W. of ALBERT (MELBOURNE TRENCH). Captain R.E.Oakley. MC & 2nd Lieut.W.Ashton joined Battalion from Training Cadre.	
	11th August		Battalion in same dispositions.	
	12th August		Battalion in same dispositions. 1st Battalion 129th Regt, U.S. Army attached to the Battalion.	
	13th August		Battalion in same dispositions. A Draft of 256 arrived, about 50 were old 2nd & 7th Battalion men - remainder first times out.	
	14th August		Night 14/15th inst. "B" & "C" Coys.relieved the 11th Royal Fusiliers in Left sub-sector 54th Bde.Front. "A" & "D" Coys. remained in MELBOURNE TRENCH. Major. L.H. Keep. MC. proceeded to Brigade as Acting Brigade Major. 12 W.O's.- C/Q.M.S. & Sergeants despatched to Base as supernumerary to establishment. Lieut. & Quartermaster F. Wombwell, Mentioned in Despatches.	
	15th August		"B" & "C" Companies relieved by 11th Royal Fusiliers & on completion relieved 6th Northamptons in Right Sub-sector, Lieut. de Buriatte Wounded - 2 O.R's wounded.	

Army Form C. 2118.

WAR DIARY
or
INTELLIGENCE SUMMARY.
(Erase heading not required.)

Instructions regarding War Diaries and Intelligence Summaries are contained in F.S. Regs., Part II. and the Staff Manual respectively. Title pages will be prepared in manuscript.

Place	Date	Hour	Summary of Events and Information.	Remarks and references to Appendices
In Field.	16th August.		"B" & "C" Companies relieved in Line by 6th Northamptons. After completion of relief "B" Coy. took up position in MELBOURNE TRENCH. "C" Company in MURRAY TRENCH. (Ref. Map. SENLIS. 1/20,000).	
	17th August.		Battalion in same dispositions. Major. L.H.Keep. MC. returned from Brigade.	
	18th August.		Battalion relieved and took over Bivouacs in HENENCOURT WOOD. Preliminary instructions were issued in the event of the Brigade going forward. The whole of the 54th Bde. & attached Units forming the Advanced Guard to the 18th Division.	
	19th August.		Dispositions as for 18th. Lieut.C.N.A.Sharland (Suffolk Regt) joined Battalion.	
	20th August.		Battalion relieved a Battalion of 47th Division as Battalion in Brigade Reserve E. of DERNANCOURT. Lieut. W.G. Samuel (Suffolk Regt) joined Battalion.	
	21st August.		Battalion in same dispositions as on 20th. Casualties:- 5 O.R's Wounded, 1 O.R. Accidentally wounded.	
	22nd August		Brigade attacked just S. of ALBERT. Captain.W.E.Aylwin MC commanding Battalion in Line vice Commanding Officer who commanded Brigade vice Brigadier, wounded. Battalion in Brigade Reserve at At night the Battalion relieved 11th Royal Fusiliers on left Sub-sector on left of TARA HILL. Casualties:- 2/Lieut.W.Whitbourn MC. Killed in Action. Lieut. G.B. Reed. Wounded. 6 O.R's - Killed in Action. 48 O.R's - Wounded. 2 O.R's - Missing. 1 O.R. - Accidentally wounded	

Army Form C. 2118.

WAR DIARY
or
INTELLIGENCE SUMMARY.
(Erase heading not required.)

Instructions regarding War Diaries and Intelligence Summaries are contained in F. S. Regs., Part II. and the Staff Manual respectively. Title pages will be prepared in manuscript.

Place	Date	Hour	Summary of Events and Information	Remarks and references to Appendices
In Field.	23rd August.		Battalion in same dispositions. Lieut. W. Harrison (Hunts Cyclists Bn) joined Battalion. Captain H.Seys-Phillips in Command of Battalion. Casualties :- Lieut. G.B. Reed. Died of Wounds. 3 O.R's Killed (attached 54th T.M.Battery). 9 O.R's Wounded.	
	24th August		Battalion in dispositions as on 23rd. Line advanced during day about 1000 yards without opposition. Casualties:- Lieut. D.P. Cross. Killed in Action. 7 O.R's - Wounded.	
	25th August.		Lt.Colonel. A.E. Percival DSO., MC. assumes command of the Battalion. Battalion took part in the attack and capture of FRICOURT, and the line was advanced about two mile. Casualties:- 3 O.R's Killed in Action. 6 O.R's Wounded 1 O.R. ; (54th T.M.Battery).	
	26th August.		54th Brigade held Line of Resistance in front of CONTALMAISON - FRICOURT ROAD. Casualties:- 2 O.R. Wounded 2nd Lieut. R.J.Vince joined Battalion. Embarked 21.8.18.	
	27th August.		54th Brigade in Div. Reserve in dispositions as on 26th inst. Casualties - 2 O.R. Wounded.	
	28th August.		Battalion relieved by 8th Bn. Royal Berks Regt. in front line - TRONES WOOD.	

Army Form C. 2118.

WAR DIARY
or
INTELLIGENCE SUMMARY.
(Erase heading not required.)

Instructions regarding War Diaries and Intelligence Summaries are contained in F. S. Regs., Part II. and the Staff Manual respectively. Title pages will be prepared in manuscript.

Place	Date	Hour	Summary of Events and Information	Remarks and references to Appendices
In Field.	29th August.		At 5.15 a.m. 38th (Welsh) Division attacked from LONGUEVAL in a S.E. direction through DELVILLE WOOD under a heavy barrage. No enemy were encountered and the Battalion advanced without opposition on the right of the 38th Division, taking GUILLEMONT. Northampton Regt on the right did not start at first but eventually conformed to the movement. The 12th Division on the Northampton's Right, did not move till late in the morning. LEUZE WOOD and the high ground to the N. of it were captured without much trouble owing to the speed of the advance although prisoners stated that the enemy intended to hold the line. Our advance was held up by strong machine gun fire from the enemy in position along the spur running from MORVAL Southwards towards COMBLES. We established a line during the day from T.16.c.3.0. to T.27.b.2.6. with a post forward about T.28.a.3.7. (Ref. Map. Sheet. 62.C. N.W. & 57. C. S.W.). Casualties:- Killed in Action. 4 O.R. Wounded in Action 34 O.R.s	
	30th August		On the morning of 30th an unsuccessful attempt was made to capture the SUNKEN ROAD running from T.16.d.8.5. to T.22.d.8.5. but as a result the line was advanced & run along the SUNKEN ROAD T.16.d.3.7. to T.22.b.4.1. & thence S. through the E. end of COMBLES. Enemy artillery was very active throughout the day and no counter-battery work was practised by our batteries. The whole forward area was strongly searched all day with all calibres. We suffered a large number of casualties in the front line as a result. At Dusk the following dispositions were taken up:- "D" Coy. Railway Cutting & Trench in T.22.a.square with liaison post about T.16.c.5.3. "A" Coy. Trench in T.22.c.square with advanced Platoon in SUNKEN RD.T.22.c.8.0.- T.22.c.8.5. "B" Coy. About T.28.d.4.8. with advanced posts about T.28.b.8.3. "C" Coy. Trench line T.27.b.5.3. to T.28.c.0.0. S.O.S.Line after 8 pm will be - T.16.d.0.2. - T.22.b.4.0.- T.22.d.8.0.- T.29.a.0.7. (Ref. Map. Sheet 62.c. N.W. & 57 C. S.W.). Casualties:- 2/Lieut. A.D. Greenwood. Killed in Action. Captain P.J.Reiss. MC. MM. Wounded remaining at duty. 9 O.R. Killed in Action. 32 O.R. Wounded. 5 O.R. Missing.	

Army Form C. 2118.

WAR DIARY
or
INTELLIGENCE SUMMARY.
(Erase heading not required.)

Place	Date	Hour	Summary of Events and Information	Remarks and references to Appendices
In Field	31st August		Before dawn 31st inst "B" Company succeeded in establishing a line of posts T.29.a.3.5. T.22.b.8.8. - QUARRY at T.22.d.6.2. - T.22.d.0.6.in touch with "D" Company. No enemy shelling during the day as enemy guns had evidently been taken back during the night. Our guns fired throughout the day and night. (Ref. Map. Sheet 62.c. N.W. & 57. c. S.W.). Casualties:- 3 Other Ranks Wounded. 3 : : Missing. Draft of 40 Other Ranks joined from Base. 2/Lieut R.W. Smith.) : H. Russell.) Joined Battalion. Embarked 21.8.18.. : J.E. Bowen.) PRISONERS: During the month of August the Battalion Captured 1 Officer and 71 Other Ranks German Prisoners.	

9.9.18.

Major.

Commanding 2nd Bn. Bedfordshire Regiment.

NARRATIVE OF OPERATIONS FROM 5th to 8th AUGUST 1918

DISPOSITIONS.   The 2nd Bedfordshire Regiment held the Brigade front from the River at P.6.a.4.6. to junction of the 55th Brigade at K.25.b.7.7. with four Companies in line, each finding their own Supports (see appendix 1.)

The Bedfords were to be relieved on the night of 5/6th by the 8th London Regt, and on completion of the relief were to take over the line of the 55th Brigade from the East Surrey Regt from K.20.a.6.9. to K.25.b.7.7.

Arrangements were made accordingly, and owing to the bad state of the trenches and the heavy shelling, guides for the incoming Units were ordered to start with their relieving Platoons from J.28.c.5.5.at 8.15 p.m., in order to get as far as possible before dark. This was essential in view of the double relief. At the last moment the incoming Brigade (174th) altered all arrangements and postponed the start till 9.30 p.m. and it was actually 10 p.m. and quite dark before the guides were able to start.   The men were very exhausted and distressed from the start, and progress was slow. At 3.30 a.m. the leading Company was stuck in the communication trench 600 yards short of the front line.
One incoming Company had relieved my right Company overland, but the other three incoming Companies were sticky and exhausted.   At this period it became obvious that the double relief could not be completed by night, and all available Officers and N.C.Os from my Battalion Headquarters were sent forward to expedite the completion of the first relief.
At 4.0 a.m. the enemy put down a heavy barrage on the old British Front Line, all communication trenches and back areas which was followed by a strong Infantry Attack at about 4.30 a.m.

SITUATION 4.45 am My two Right Companies had been relieved and were moving to their new positions in Support in COOLGARDIE TRENCH and COBAR TRENCH N. of the COOTAMUNDRA TRENCH (communication) in the 55th Brigade Area.   My two left Companies had not been completely relieved. There was no communication with Companies except by Runner, and it took more than one hour to get a message forward.

OPERATIONS.   The enemy captured my Outpost Line between K.25.b.7.7. and K.25.c.5.5. and penetrated deeply on the front of the Battalion on my left (East Surreys) particularly on the BRAY-CORBIE road where a quarry at J.24.b.8.8. was entered by the enemy and prisoners taken.

My two left Companies holding the original British Front Line from K.25.b.2.8. to J.30.d.8.4. put up a very strong resistance which prevented any further penetration, counter-attacked on their own initiative and regained the Outpost Line K.25.c.0.4. to K.25.c. central which was handed over to the London Regt.   My Supporting Companies with the East Surreys' Stragglers cleared up the situation in J.24.b and occupied COBAR LINE intact.

At 6.0 a.m. I was holding CUMMINS TRENCH from K.19.d.4.1. to my junction with the London Regt. on my right inclusive, which position was maintained until relieved by the 36th Brigade on the night of 7/8th.

During the 6th my Support Company moved a Platoon into CRUMP LANE. Local Fighting took place during the 6th and all positions were maintained and improved.

continued.

COUNTER-ATTACK. At dawn on the 7th acting under Brigade Orders, three Platoons of my Reserve Company Counter)attacked in conjunction with the Northamptons on my left and regained the original British Front Line at K.19.d.8.8. where connection was established with the Battalion on the Left. This point was exclusive to my Battalion. Local and confused fighting took place during the 7th but my positions were always maintained and touch kept with the Northamptons in CONAMULLA SUPPORT. During this fighting the spirit of the men under my Command was excellent. ~~During this fighting th~~ The enemy presented numerous targets of which full advantage was taken by all ranks.

About 3.0 a.m. on the 8th the Battalion was relieved by the Royal Sussex Regt. of the 36th Brigade, and my outposts were withdrawn about 3.30 a.m.

REMARKS. The state of the forward trenches and communication trenches cannot be realized by those who were not present.

Enemy Artillery prevented movement of bodies of troops over the top. Communications were bad on the 6th but better on the 7th.

CASUALTIES.   8 Officers   163 Other Ranks.
SICK WASTAGE.   1 Officer   80 Other Ranks. (approx)

EFFECTIVES ON THE 7th inst.   In four Companies (6.0 a.m.)
                   8 Officers   190 Other Ranks.

Artillery support was indifferent at first but subsequently improved.

Army Form C. 2118.

WAR DIARY
or
INTELLIGENCE SUMMARY.
(Erase heading not required.)

Instructions regarding War Diaries and Intelligence Summaries are contained in F.S. Regs., Part II. and the Staff Manual respectively. Title pages will be prepared in manuscript.

Place	Date	Hour	Summary of Events and Information	Remarks and references to Appendices
In the Field	1.9.18.		Battalion in dispositions at T.20.d.2.4. in Divisional Reserve. Casualties:- 1 O.R. Killed., 1 O.R. Died of Wounds. 117 P.O.W. Captured by Bn.	
	2.9.18.		Battalion at T.20.d.2.4. Resting.	
	3.9.18.		Battalion at T.20.d.2.4. Resting.	
	4.&9.18.		Battalion at T.20.d.2.4. Training.	
	5.9.18.		Battalion at T.20.d.2.4. Training.	
	6.9.18.		Battalion at T.20.d.2.4. Training.	
	7.9.18.		Battalion at T.20.d.2.4. Training. Major.L.H.Keep. M.C. took over command of Battalion vice Lt.Colonel.A.M.Percival DSO.,MC. to Reserve. 19 Other Ranks from Base.	
	8.9.18.		Battalion at T.20.d.2.4. Training. The following awards were notified:- Bar to Military Medal:- 18617 Sgt.D.Fynn. MM. 14583 Sgt.E.T.Blake. MM. 3/2572 Pte.F.Dunton. Military Medal:- 40813 ; W.G Ashby.	
	9.9.18.		Battalion at T.20.d.2.4. Training. Lieutenant.D.F.Howard appointed Intelligence officer, 54th Bde & Struck off strength.	
	10.9.18.		Battalion at T.20.d.2.4. Training. The III Corps Commander presented ribbons on a presentation parade to the undermentioned. 17442 Pte.A.Cradliffe. DCM. 14293 Pte.T.Moss. M.M. 23796 Cpl.A.Clifton. M.M 3/2572 Pte. F.Dunton. M.M. 40813 Pte.W.G.Ashby. M.M. 18917 Sgt. D.Fynn. Bar to M.M. Captain. H. Boys-Phillips. Croix de Guerre.	
	11.9.18.		Battalion at T.20.d.2.4. Training.	

Army Form C. 2118.

WAR DIARY
or
INTELLIGENCE SUMMARY.
(Erase heading not required.)

Instructions regarding War Diaries and Intelligence Summaries are contained in F. S. Regs., Part II and the Staff Manual respectively. Title pages will be prepared in manuscript.

Place	Date	Hour	Summary of Events and Information	Remarks and references to Appendices
In the Field	12.9.18.		Battalion at T.20.d.2.4. Training.	
	13.9.18.		Battalion at T.20.d.2.4. Training. 3 O.R. T.M.Battery accidentally wounded. Draft 14 O.R. from Base.	
	14.9.18.		Battalion at T.20.d.2.4. Training.	
	15.9.18.		Battalion at T.20.d.2.4. Training.	
	16.9.18.		Battalion embussed at LEUZE WOOD & proceeded to a wood W. of AIZECOURT-LE-BAS. 2nd Lieut. W. Pennington joined Battalion.	See Appendix 1
	17.9.18.		Battalion in same position. In the evening Battalion moved to assembly position W. of RONSSOY.	See Appendix II
	18.9.18.		Battalion took part in attack on RONSSOY. Lieut.A.E.Ogle. Wounded. 2/Lieut.H.Russell. wounded. 2/Lieut.S.E.Dancer. Wounded. 2/Lieut.J.Kerr. Wounded. Lieut.W.S.Oliver.Jones.Wounded. Draft 12 O.R. from Base.	See Appendix III & map.
	19.9.18.		Battalion took part in Operations near RONSSOY. Lieut.J.M.Glen. Wounded. Lieut.S.E.D.Cline wounded., 2/Lieut.W.R.Smith. Wounded at duty. Major.I.H.Keep. MC. Wounded & at duty.	
	20.9.18.		Battalion took part in Operations near RONSSOY.	
	21.9.18.		Battalion took part in operations near RONSSOY. Lieut.W.G.Saddle. Killed., Lieut.S.G.Neggs. Died of Wounds. Lieut.H.B.Stow.&.NC.Wounded. 2/Lieut.J.C.Bowen. Wounded., 2/Lieut.W.R.Smith.Missing., Captain.E.E.Gett. wounded. 2/Lieut.D.Davies. Wounded.	
	22.9.18.		Battalion took part in operations near RONSSOY. Lieut.R.W.Oldfield.MC. Wounded & at duty. Lieut.W.R.Harrison.Wounded & at duty. Total Casualties up to 12 mn. during operations from 18th – 22.9.18. Officers. O.R. Killed - 1 48 Missing - 1 17 Wounded 11 175 Died of wds. M.1	

Army Form C. 2118.

WAR DIARY
or
INTELLIGENCE SUMMARY.
(Erase heading not required.)

Instructions regarding War Diaries and Intelligence Summaries are contained in F.S. Regs., Part II. and the Staff Manual respectively. Title pages will be prepared in manuscript.

Place	Date	Hour	Summary of Events and Information	Remarks and references to Appendices
In the Field	22.9.18.		Lt.Colonel. A.E.Percival. DSO.,MC. from leave.	
	23.9.18.		Battalion took part in operations near RONSSOY. The Battalion were relieved by 7th Bn.R.W.Kents Regt. at midnight. and marched to QUARRY near ST EMILIE.	
	24.9.18.		Battalion in quarry about 100 yards W. of ST EMILE, Resting.	
	25.9.18.		Battalion marched to billets near NURLU.	
	26.9.18.		Battalion at NURLU re-organizing & refitting 2nd Lieut. D.Davies awarded M.C.	
	27.9.18.		Battalion at NURLU re-organising & refitting.	
	28.9.18.		Battalion proceeded to Area W. of EPEHY. Draft 20 O.R. from Base. (see O.O. 35).	
	29.9.18.		Operations near RONSSOY WOOD. Casualties 2 O.R. Killed in Action.. 19 O.R. Wounded. Brigade attacked & captured the KNOLL E. of RONSSOY forming left flank to Americans. Battalion in Reserve except "A" Coy. under command of Lieut.R.I.Edwards. MC. attached to a Battalion of Americans to do liaison work. "B" & "C" Coys employed as carrying parties. "D" Company formed "Mopping up" Company. Battalion Hd qrs W. of RONSSOY WOOD (c.8.b.)	
	30.9.18.		"B" & "C" Coys. were ordered to proceed to VENDHUILLE as mopping up Coys.but did not arrive as village was not captured. Battalion relieved 11th Royal Fusiliers in the Line & cleared the village of VENDHUILLE up to the Canal. 2/Lieut.H.B.Lang., 2/Lieut. H. Hyslop., 2/Lieut. C.J.Sturges., 2/Lieut.L.L.Whittingham joined Battalion from Base.	

2.10.18.

A.E.Percival
Lt.Colonel.
Commanding 2rd Bn. Bedfordshire Regiment.

SECRET

Appendix I

2nd Bn. Bedfordshire Regt.   Operation Order No. 53

B.E.F. .... 15.9.18.   Copy No. 12

Reference SHEET 62c. N.E.

1. The Battalion will move tomorrow by bus to NURLU and thence by march route to billets in the AIZECOURT LE BAS Area.

2. The Transport will move by march route under the Brigade Transport Officer at 7.0 a.m.

3. The Battle Surplus will be under the command of Captain R.L.V. Doake. MC. and will be accomodated near FAVIERES WOOD in A.5.d. They will remain in their present billets till orders are received from Captain Doake.

4. The Battalion will probably embus at 10.0 a.m. on the GUILLEMONT - COMBLES ROAD.
One N.C.O. per Company & Headquarters will assist Lieut. C.H. Hart to embus the Battalion. Further instructions will be issued when received.

5. <u>Dress</u>. Battle Order, blanket rolled in waterproof sheet and carried round the haversack.

6. Lewis Guns and Drums being taken into battle will be carried, also dixies used for breakfast.

7. Company Commanders will proceed by bus leaving Brigade H.Q. at 9.0 a.m. to reconnoitre the Forward Area.

8. Officers Valises will be dumped as follows:-
H.Qrs. "A" & "D" Coys. at Hd.Qrs. by 8.50 a.m.
"B" & "C" Coys. by 9.0 a.m. at "B" Coys. H.Q.

9. Quartermaster Stores & Transport Lines will be located at A.23.d.

10. All tents will be struck by the Battle Surplus and handed in to the Q.M. Stores as soon as possible after the Battalion has left them.

11. <u>ACKNOWLEDGE</u>.

H. Seys Phillips

Captain & A/Adjutant.
2nd Battalion Bedfordshire Regt.

Copies to: No. 1. C.O.   6. D. Coy.
            2. Adjutant.   7. Quartermaster.
            3. A. Coy.   8. Transport Officer
            4. B. Coy.   9. Medical Officer
            5. C. Coy.   10. R.S.M.
                                11. 54th Bde.
                                12. War Diary
                                13. File.

MESSAGE FORM

_____ Division

_____ Map Reference or Mark
                  on Map at Back.

1. I am at _____
2. I am at _____ and am consolidating
3. I am at _____ and have consolidated.
4. Am held up by M.G. at _____
5. I need: Ammunition
             Bombs
             Rifle Grenades
             Water
             Verey Lights
             Stokes Shells
6. Counter-attack forming up at _____
7. I am in touch with _____ on Right at _____
                                        on Left at _____
8. I am not in touch on Right
                       Left
9. _____
10. I estimate my present strength at _____ rifles.
11. Hostile {Battery   } active at _____
            {Machine Gun }
            {Trench Mortar}

Time _____ m   Name _____
                   Platoon _____
Date _____   Company _____
                   Battalion _____

2nd Bedfords

2 Bedfords
04.44

46.9
14 attack

OPERATION ORDER No.55
By
Major L.H.Keep, M.C.,
Commanding 2nd Bn. Bedfordshire Regiment,
17/9/18.

SECRET.

-:-:-:-:-:-:-:-:-:-:-:-:-:-:-:-:-

1. The Battalion in conjunction with the 24th Welsh Regiment on the right will attack, capture and consolidate the Southern portion of ROUSSOY Village, on the 18th as per special map issued herewith.

2. The Battalion will assemble two hours before Zero in Company Areas in F.19.Central as already indicated on the ground.
   The Battalion will move forward from its forming up line at ZERO plus 15. Coys will move in Artillery Formation and will maintain this formation as long as possible until they pick up their own shrapnel barrage which must be followed closely.

3. ZERO HOUR will be notified later.

4. Battalion Headquarters will be situated at E.18.c.9/6 and will subsequently move forward to a position to be notified later.

5. R.A.P. will be at Battalion Headquarters.

6. The forward end of the Loop Set will go forward with "D" Company.

7. DRESS:- BATTLE ORDER, with shovels, picks, smoke bombs, and Bombs.

8. The 7th Bn.R.W.Kent.Regt, will make the initial attack on the Brigade Frontage under a shrapnel barrage as far as a Line from F.21.b.5/0 to F.15.d.5/5., which they will reach at ZERO plus 56 minutes.

9. At ZERO plus 58 minutes the 2nd Bn.Bedfordshire Regt will pass through the West Kents and continue the attack as far as a line from F.23.a.0/0 to F.17/a.0/0., where they will consolidate and mop up by areas as per special Map.

10. Order of Battle. "B" Coy on the right assaulting on a frontage of 400 yards from F.19.d.6/5 to F.19.b.6/5.
    "C" Company assaulting on the left from F.19.b.6/5 to F.13.d.6/1.
    "D" Coy will be in support to "B" Coy and "A" Coy in support to "C" Coy.
    O.C. Supporting Companies will each keep one platoon in reserve.

11. Role of Coys:- All Companies will fight their way through and mop up and consolidate the areas shown on special maps. Tanks will co-operate.

12. At ZERO plus 116 the 11th R.Fusiliers and 6th Northamptons will form up facing North on a line from (R.Fusrs) F.16.c.9/7 (COLLEEN POST to F.15.d.8/6. (6th N'Hants) F.15.d.8/6 to F.15.c.Central and attack Northwards under an enfilade shrapnel barrage in co-operation with troops on their Left.

CONTINUED.

C.O.No.35 (Continued).

13. Liaison Posts:- "B" Coy - Post on Sunken Road at N.E. Corner of Wood (F.28.a.8/0., with Welsh Battalion.
"C" Company COLLEEN POST with R.Fusrs.
"A" Coy - Cross Roads F.15.d.8/8 with Fusiliers and Northamptons.

14. Two Stokes Mortars will be attached to "A" Coy for the purpose of clearing their Liaison Post.
Machine Gun arrangements will be notified later.

15. Acknowledge.

[signature]

Captain
A/Adjutant 2nd Bn. Bedfordshire Regiment.

Copy No.1 to C.O.
2 Adjutant.
3 54th Bde.
4 O.C. "A" Coy.
5 O.C. "B" Coy.
6 O.C. "C" Coy.
7 O.C. "D" Coy.
8 O.C. 11th R.Fusrs.
9 O.C. 6th N'Hants.
10 O.C. 24th Welsh Regt.
11 O.C. 54t T.M.B.
12 Qr.Mr.
13 Tpt.Offr.
14 M.O.
15 File.
16 War Diary
17 -:-

War Diary
[illegible]
30-9-18

Map Sheet 62c N.E. & 62d N.W.

1. The Battalion [will attack positions?] immediately to the line of trenches between A.7.b.15.35 and A.7.d.9.9 [tomorrow morning?] in conjunction with the troops on right and left. The first operation will be attack on the left and 74th Div. on right.

2. The Battalion will attack on a two company front. D Coy will be assaulting Company and will take the line of trenches between F.12.c.5.2 and F.19.d.95.70. A Company will then pass through to the final objective as above.

3. B Company will be in Support and C Company in Reserve.

4. The Battalion will be formed up by 3 a.m. The position of the forming up line will be noted later. B Company will be in SHAMROCK TRENCH and the trench about F.12.c.9.2.
C Company will be in D Company's old trench in F.12.a.[?]

5. Battalion Hd.Qrs. will move to "C" Company's old Hd. Qrs. at F.21.b.8.6. at 10 p.m. One hour after Zero, if the situation permits, an advanced report centre will be established at DUNCAN POST.

6. The advance will be under a shrapnel barrage, further particulars of which will be issued when received.
   Tanks will co-operate in latter stages of the attack.

7. A Company will not pass through "D" Coy. on to the Final Objective until the "Knoll" has been captured and the Tanks have come down into the Valley in A.7.b. & d.

8. Success signals will be fired on the capture of each objective.

9. Zero hour will be notified later.

10. ACKNOWLEDGE

H. Phillips
Capt & A/ Adjutant
2nd Bn. Bedfordshire Regt.

Copy No. 1. C.O.   No. 2. 54th Bde.
3-6. O.C. Coys.   7-8. War Diary

REPORT ON OPERATIONS 20TH/22ND SEPTEMBER 1918

At dawn on morning of 20th the 2nd Bedfords attacked in a North Easterly direction from the BELLICOURT ROAD in conjunction with the 74th Division on Right and 6th Northamptons on Left in order to obtain distant objectives.

Before Zero the assembly positions were heavily shelled and at Zero the enemy's barrage came down very rapidly and with great intensity on our assaulting troops being particularly severe in the Valley, F.23.a.

The situation was obscure until 9.0 a.m. when all troops were found to be very much mixed and the following information was obtained.

About 20 men and 1 Officer and 3 Vickers Guns of 54th Brigade at QUENCHETTES WOOD, F.23.b.1.6. About 80 men at HOLLAND POST, F.17.b.6.3. SART FARM reported held by Brigade on our Left. Other troops were known to be well forward on our flanks but no exact information was obtainable. The Quadralateral DUNCAN POST, MILL LANE, DOG TRENCH, POT LANE, DUNCAN AVENUE was seen to be strongly held by the enemy.

At 10.0 a.m. after reconnoitring approaches to HOLLAND POST I ordered my Reserve Company to form up in SUNKEN ROAD West of HOLLAND POST and in conjunction with troops in this area to rush and capture the trench system between DOLEFUL POST and DUNCAN POST covered by Machine Gun and Rifle Fire. This attack was attempted at 11.30 a.m. but met with no success.

Situation Mid-day. Bedfords and Northamptons had no reserves, Communication with advanced troops was difficult. Casualties and particularly Officer Casualties were known to be severe and the enemy was in a commanding position on high ground on our front. I was unable to get any exact information from the 74th Division but it was known that their advanced troops had been counter-attacked and were falling back slowly. Nothing was known of the situation on my left until later in the afternoon when the Northamptons reported that they held a section of trench about DOLEFUL POST.

I reported the situation to you and received instructions for a further attack on the RED LINE to take place at 12.15 mn. for which purpose a Composite Company of 11th Royal Fusiliers were attached to my Battalion and assembled on the BELLICOURT ROAD. At dusk my Reserve Company was collected and brought back to original starting position.

NIGHT ATTACK

At Midnight in conjunction with troops on my Right, 1 Company 11th Royal Fusiliers attacked DUNCAN POST after a sharp bombardment but unfortunately lost direction and after sharp fighting secured a number of prisoners and a trench position which they reported incorrectly as being DUNCAN POST and stated that they were in touch with troops on their Right but their Left Flank was exposed. The 74th Division had previously reported that they held the Quadralateral at MILL LANE, POT TRENCH, DOG TRENCH, CAT POST.

A daylight reconnaissance showed that the Fusiliers had passed through the 74th Division and captured CAT POST and a portion of DOG TRENCH and POT LANE, all the remainder were held by the enemy.

Continued.

OPERATIONS

I immediately organised a further attack with all available troops under my Command in conjunction with "B" Coy. M.G.Corps, Advanced Sections "C" Battery, 110 Army Brigade, and our own Artillery and reported situation to you. Difficulty was experienced in co-operating with 74th Division owing to lack of communication and indifferent liaison. At 3.0 p.m. all available artillery were to bombard DUNCAN AVENUE for 10 inutes when DUNCAN POST was to be stormed and captured by troops co-operating on both flanks. 30 Bedfords had previously joined the Northamptons in DOLEFUL TRENCH and prolonged their Right Flank which was still unsupported. 20 Prisoners were captured in this operation.

At 2.30 p.m. the enemy were observed assembling for a Counter-attack on my front and left front in F.17.d. and F.18.a.

I ordered my Reserve Company to pass through 74th Division via BENJAMIN POST and CAT POST and attack from MILL LANE which was reported to be held by 74th Division. The troops of 54th Brigade were to attack from South West from F.23.b.1.6. and the remainder of my Battalion were to attack down trench from F.17.b.

At 3.0 p.m. the Divisional Artillery failed to materialize but the Advanced Section of "C" Battery, 110 Brigade, made excellent shooting on DUNCAN AVENUE and at 3.10 p.m. troops of this Brigade well led and handled by their Subordinate Commanders, advanced engaged, defeated and surrounded the enemy, and in so doing cleared DOG TRENCH, MILL LANE, POT TRENCH, POT LANE, DUNCAN AVENUE and DUNCAN POST. About 400 of the enemy were in this Area of whom about 100 attempted to escape by Sunken Roads (FLEET STREET and VALE STREET) pursued over the open by men of 11th Royal Fusiliers from CAT POST.

3.45 p.m. In reply to our S.O.S. and intense barrage came down in front of our line completely annihilating a prepared German Counter-attack on DOLEFUL POST. The enemy were estimated to be 600 strong and were caught by cross Machine Gun and Rifle fire in front and our shrapnel barrage behind and failed to reach our trenches where our men were taking full advantage of the best living target one could hope to see. Prisoners were taken.

On our right our barrage caught the retreating Germans and unfortunately the pursuing Royal Fusiliers who fell back to CAT POST, DOG TRENCH.

Situation. 35 men mostly Bedfords and a few Northamptons under 2 Officers had surrounded about 300 of the enemy and had cleared and were garrisoning 800 yards of enemy trench. The mopping up proceeded but this Brigade were unable to spare men for escort and it is believed that most of the prisoners passed through 74th Division Cage from 4.0 p.m. onwards.

About 100 prisoners were assembled about my Battalion Hd.Qrs. and sent to the rear. Northamptons on left and 74th Division assembled others. Number of Prisoners believed to have been captured in this operation - 150/200. Estimated number of Germans killed 200.
NOTE - 80 Germans dead and 30 Machine Guns were found in DUNCAN POST. alone.

Bedfords and Northamptons in F.17.b. were too busily engaged in repulsing German Counter-attack to co-operate in this movement but they subsequently gained touch with my troops at F.17.d.5.8. about 7.0 p.m. when for the first time since Zero on previous day a definite line was established on Brigade front.

contd.

-3-

The men employed in this successful operation were in very good heart and immediately consolidated the line gained in which they were ably assisted by the 80th Field Company, R.E. under Captain Weir who proceeded to wire DUNCAN POST within a very few hours of its capture. DUNCAN AVENUE in F.18.c. was exploited and gave further prisoners.

About Midnight troops in this Area were relieved by 55th Infantry Brigade.

Casualties in carrying out this operation were as follows:-

Bedfords } 2 Killed, 7 wounded.
Northamptons)

Royal Fusiliers. 15 wounded by our S.O.S. barrage.

"B" Coy. M.G. Corps. 1 wounded.

In my opinion success of this operation was entirely due to the resolution and vigour with which attack was pressed by Lieut. Oldfield and his party of 14 men from F.23.b.1.6. and 2/Lieut. Pennington and his party of 30 from MILL LANE and for the speed with which the 11th Royal Fusiliers pursued the enemy from their position in CAT POST.

"B" Company, Machine Gun Corps ably assisted by direct fire with 4 guns from F.23.b.1.6. as arranged with Major Burns.

The support of the Advanced Section of "C" Battery 110 Army Brigade was invaluable and the shooting was exceedingly accurate.

The men employed used their rifles freely and by always adopting the boldest policy the subordinate and Section Commanders secured immediate and material results with a minimum of casualties.

REMARKS

Throughout these operations communications were difficult and indifferent, Runner and Lamp being the only reliable means. Power Buzzer was useful at times. Loop Set was generally out of order and the Wire was frequently disconnected.

Liaison with Division on Right was difficult. Information received from other sourses was not always reliable.

The enemy did not surrender freely until he was completely surrounded and even then only under pressure.

25.8.18.

Major.
Commanding 2nd Battalion Bedfordshire Regiment,

WAR DIARY or INTELLIGENCE SUMMARY

Army Form C. 2118.

(*Erase heading not required.*)

Place	Date	Hour	Summary of Events and Information	Remarks and references to Appendices
	1st to 31st Oct. 1918.			
	1st October.		Battalion engaged in operations near VENDHUILLE. Draft of 39 O.R. from Base. 2nd Lieuts. C.J.VOWLES, C.L.TOOLEY, T.F.VAUGHAN joined battalion. 1 O.R. Killed, 1 O.R. Wounded, 2nd Lt.G.B.PHIPPS ceased to be attached to 1ith Bn.R.Fusrs. Battalion were relieved in the front line by the Scottish Horse (50th Div) and proceeded to RONSSOY.	
	2nd October.		Battalion embussed and proceeded to PIERREGOT (Ref.Map.LENS 11). "D" Company were detached as Burial Party.	
	3rd October.		Battalion at PIERREGOT. 2nd Lt.A.F.ALDRIDGE, Lieut.H.D.CHESTER, 2nd Lieuts. W.K.G.HARDING, W.F.S.WILFORD,M.M. and B.H.SAINSBURY joined Battalion.	
	4th October.		Battalion at PIERREGOT.	
	5th October.		Battalion at PIERREGOT. Lieut.A.P.METHUEN, A.J.WHITWORTH and 2ndLieuts. J.E.STUTCHBURY and H.DYSART joined Battalion from Base. Lieut.A.P.METHUEN appointed Assistant Adjutant. Draft of 153 O.R. from base.	
	6th October.		Battalion at PIERREGOT - Resting. 2nd Lt.W.TYSOE, D.S.O., appointed Battalion Intelligence Officer.	
	7th October.		Battalion at PIERREGOT - Training - Section and Platoon Drill and Lewis Gun Instruction.	
	8th October.		Battalion at PIERREGOT Training. 2nd Lieuts W.T.HALL, S.H.ABBOTT, W.H.RIDGEWELL, and W.H.WALDOCK from Base. Lieut.C.N.A.SHARLAND to England Sick 26.9.18 and struck off strength.	
	9th October.		Battalion at PIERREGOT Training.	
	10th October.		Battalion at PIERREGOT - Training.	
			Continued.	

Army Form C. 2118.

WAR DIARY
or
INTELLIGENCE SUMMARY
(Erase heading not required.)

Instructions regarding War Diaries and Intelligence Summaries are contained in F. S. Regs., Part II. and the Staff Manual respectively. Title Pages will be prepared in manuscript.

Place	Date	Hour	Summary of Events and Information	Remarks and references to Appendices
	1st to 31st Oct. 1918.			
	11th October.		Battalion at PIERREGOT Training.	
	12th October.		Battalion at PIERREGOT - Brigade Sports - Battalion won 9 out of 15 events. 2nd Lieut.W.ASHTON and S.W.GOBLE awarded the MILITARY CROSS.	
	13th October.		Battalion at PIERREGOT. Capt.W.E.AYLWIN, M.C. to England Sick.	
	14th October.		Battalion at PIERREGOT - Training. Orders received to be ready to move by Tactical Train at 24 hours notice.	
	15th October.		Battalion at PIERREGOT Training. Battalion won 18th Div.Cross Country Race - 20 Starters per Battalion, first 15 to count.	
	16th October.		Battalion at PIERREGOT Training. No.25466 Pte.S.J.Harris awarded the Military Medal. Transport moved off in afternoon for forward areas.	
	17th October.		Battalion marched to POULAINVILLE and entrained for ROISEL. On arrival at ROISEL the Battalion marched to NURLU.	
	18th October.		Battalion embussed at Cross Roads on PERONNE - NURLU Road and proceeded to SERAIN.	
	19th October.		Battalion at SERAIN. In the afternoon the Battalion proceeded by march route to MAUROIS. Captain R.E.OAKLEY,M.C., classified B.ii and S.O.S.	
	20th October.		Battalion at MAUROIS. At 7.30 p.m. Battalion proceeded to front line and relieved 18th Bn.Kings Liverpool Regt. "B" Coy relieved "A" Coy K.L.R. from K.29.d.4.5 to K.29.c.9.9. "C" Coy relieved "D" Coy K.L.R. from K.29.c.9.9. (crossing inclusive), "C" Coy relieved "D" Coy "C" Coy K.L.R. from K.29.c.9.9. (exclusive) to K.23.c.10.25. "D" Coy relieved "B" Coy K.L.R. in cellars about road junction in K.28.d.6.8. "A" Coy relieved "B" Coy K.L.R. Bn.Hd.Qrs at K.25.a.1.4. (Ref.Map Sheet 57.B.). Casualties 2 O.R. Wounded. No.18589 Pte.T.PEARCE awarded BAR to M.M. No.33651 Pte.D.Draper awarded M.M. Continued.	

Army Form C. 2118.

WAR DIARY
or
INTELLIGENCE SUMMARY

(Erase heading not required.)

Instructions regarding War Diaries and Intelligence Summaries are contained in F.S. Regs., Part II. and the Staff Manual respectively. Title Pages will be prepared in manuscript.

Place	Date	Hour	Summary of Events and Information	Remarks and references to Appendices
1st to 31st Oct. 1918	21st October.		Battalion in Line. 2nd Lt.B.H.SAINSBURY Wounded. 1 O.R.Killed, 7 O.R. Wd.	
	22nd October.		Battalion in Line.	
	23rd October.		Battalion in Line. Operations N.E. of LE CATEAU. SEE APPENDIX 1. Casualties:- Lt.C.H.HART,Killed in Action. 2nd Lt.C.J.VOWLES Wounded. 2nd Lt.W.F.S.WILFORD,MM., Wounded and 2nd Lt.W.ASHTON,M.C., Wounded at Duty.	
	24th October.		Battalion in Line. Operations N.E. of LE CATEAU. Casualties. Capt.P.J.REISS, M.C., M.M. Wounded. 2nd Lts H.DYSART and W.C.HALL Wounded. Casualties Other Ranks during operations 20th to 24th October,1918:- 40 O.R. Killed. 169 wounded. 9 Missing. 8 Wounded and at duty. 5 O.R. Died of Wounds. Estimated prisoners captured 100. One 4.2. and 2 77 mm guns captured. One T.M.Captured. 60 Machine Guns and 2 Anti-Tank Rifles captured. Lieut.W.J.HOLBROOK, M.C. from England, 2nd Lieut.A.S.A.NIXON from England.	
	25th October.		Battalion at L'EPINETTE FARM. 2nd Lt.W.F.S.WILFORD,M.M. Died of Wounds. 2nd Lieut.S.A.G.Hill joined Battalion. Draft 7 O.R. from Base.	
	26th October.		Battalion at L'EPINETTE FARM. The Battalion relieved 8th Bn.E.Surrey Regt in the Right Brigade Sub-Sector in Brigade Reserve. Relief completed by 12 noon (SEE APPENDIX 11). 3 O.R. Wounded.	
	27th October.		Battalion in RESERVE near BOUSIES.	
	28th October.		Battalion in RESERVE near BOUSIES.	
	29th October.		Battalion in Right Sector, Front Line, near BOUSIES. "A" and "C" Coys front line, "B" and "D" Coys Support; (SEE APPENDIX 111). Draft of 6 O.R. from Base.	

Continued.

Army Form C. 2118.

WAR DIARY
or
INTELLIGENCE SUMMARY

(Erase heading not required.)

Place	Date	Hour	Summary of Events and Information	Remarks and references to Appendices
	1st to 31st Oct. 1918.			
	30th October.		Battalion were relieved by 2nd Bn.R.Munster Fusiliers and side stepped on relief to the left and relieved 6th Bn.Northamptonshire Regiment in front line. Dispositions:- "D" Coy Right, "B" Company Left. "A" and "C" Coys in Support. "A" Right "C" Left. 2nd Lieut.J.E.STUTCHBURY Wounded. 1 O.R. Killed and 4 O.R. Wounded. (SEE APPENDIX IV)	
	31st October.		Dispositions as on 30th inst. Draft 6 O.R. from Base. APPENDIX V. Congratulatory messages.	

4.11.18.

W. R____

Lt.Colonel

Commanding 2nd Bn.Bedfordshire Regiment.

War Diary Appendix 1

2nd Bn. Bedfordshire Regiment.

NARRATIVE OF OPERATIONS N.E. OF LE CATEAU - 23rd/24th OCTOBER, 1918.

Reference Sheet:- 57 B, N.E. and 57 A. N.W., 1/20,000.

PRELIMINARY MOVEMENTS.

The 2nd Bn. Bedfordshire Regt. relieved the 18th Bn. Kings Liverpool Regiment in the front line N.E. of LE CATEAU on the evening of 20th October with a view to carrying out an attack on the enemy position opposite this front. The Line taken over ran along the RAILWAY EMBANKMENT from the RICHEMONT BROOK to the Level Crossing on the LE CATEAU - RICHEMONT ROAD, and thence in a S.E. direction for 400 yards. The latter part of the Line was handed over to the 10th Bn. Essex Regiment early on the evening of 22nd October, 1918.

THE PLAN.

The Battalion was detailed to lead the attack for the 54th Inf. Bde. and the objective given was the Orchard S.E. of FOREST L.7.b and d Squares (inclusive) and thence along the Road to L.13.b.8.3., which was our Southern boundary. We received permission from the 33rd Division who were attacking on our LEFT to use the ground up to the MONTAY - FOREST Road for the purpose of forming up and manoeuvre. It was decided to launch the main attack along the high ground N. of RICHEMONT MILL and a subsidiary attack South of the MILL, the big valley running N.E. from RICHEMONT MILL being left empty, but subjected to heavy artillery and M.G. Barrages.

I accordingly detailed Companies as under:-

"C" Company under Lieut. H.D. CHESTER was to lead the attack N. of the BROOK forming up 200 yards East of the Railway, the objective given to this Coy was RICHEMONT MILL and the three Gullies N. and N.E. of it and the High Ground about K.23.b.8.7.

"A" Company under Lieut C.H. HART, was to form up behind "C" Company and also E. of the Railway and was to move along the high ground N. of the Gullies. Two Platoons were to go to the sunken road running N.E. from WHITE SPRING and two Platoons were to go to the practice trenches about L.13 Central.

"D" Company under Capt. P.J. REISS, M.C., M.M., were to form up behind "A" Company but West of the Railway and follow "A" Company passing through them on the line of the WHITE SPRINGS and going on to the final objective.

"B" Company under 2nd Lieut. H.B. LANG were to form up South of the RICHEMONT BROOK just E. of the Railway and attacking in an E.N.E. Direction were to establish themselves on the slopes of the Hill about K.24.b.Central.

Two Tanks were allotted to the Battalion, one being detailed to proceed with "A" Company and one with "D" Company.

THE ATTACK.

ZERO HOUR was fixed for 1.20 a.m. 23.10.18 and at 11 p.m. the Battalion started to move into position. Tapes had previously been put out by 2nd Lieut. V. TYSOE, D.S.O., the Battalion Intelligence Officer, for the Southern Attack and by "C" Coys Officers for the Northern Attack.

The work of forming up was carried out successfully in spite of two heavy bursts of hostile Artillery Fire at 11.15 p.m. and 12.15 a.m. and by 12.45 a.m. the Battalion was reported in position.

Battalion Headquarters had moved to the Railway Embankment K.29.a.5/4.

The night was moonlight with thick ground mist in the Valleys which made direction difficult to keep.

A very heavy barrage opened at 1.20 a.m. and at 1.24 a.m. the Companies commenced to move forward.

"C" Company had little difficulty in capturing the first two Gullies, but experienced considerable opposition from M.G. fire in crossing the high ground to attack the third Gully and suffered Casualties. Here the attack was temporarily held up but good leading by Lieut. H.D. CHESTER and 2nd Lieut. W. ASHTON, M.C., got the Company going again and the third Gully was then cleared and the Company's objective reached.

Meanwhile "A" Company had been moving North of the Gullies and after suffering some opposition and Casualties about K.18.c.0.0., where Lieut. C.H. HART was killed, the Company pushed on to their objectives. A large number of the enemy were encountered in the Sunken Road running N.W. from WHITE SPRING and heavy fighting took place here, many of the enemy being killed. All four platoons eventually reached their

objectives/

"D" Company had become involved in the fighting about the RICHEMONT MILL gullies early in the attack but Capt.REISS managed to detach half a platoon under 2nd Lieut.W.H.WALDOCK and send them forward with a Tank. This party reached their final objective about L.7.b.5.2., under the barrage. Later on Capt.REISS was able to collect the rest of his Company and led them forward to their objective.

In the meantime "B" Company, South of the RICHEMONT BROOK, had encountered considerable opposition right at the Start from Enemy M.G's who were located inside our Barrage. The Company was held up for some time and it was entirely due to the splendid leadership displayed by 2nd Lieut.H.B.LANG and other Officers and N.C.O's, who led the men forward in face of intense Machine Gun Fire and Bayoneted the gunners, that the Company was got going again. The Barrage had been lost but by sheer determination the Company fought its way forward, crossed the brook, and arrived on its final objective soon after its scheduled time. I consider the greatest credit due to 2nd Lieut.H.B. LANG and his Company for reaching their objective in spite of such strong opposition.

A subsequent examination of the ground showed the Hill both North and South of RICHEMONT MILL to have been very thickly held by a large number of Light and Heavy Machine Guns.

By 5 a.m. all Companies were reported on their final objective. The Battalions Casualties up to this time were :-

Lieutenant C.H.HART   -   Killed.
2nd Lieut.C.J.VOWLES   -   Wounded
2nd Lieut.W.F.S.WILFORD,M.M.Wounded, Died of Wds 25.10.18.
2rd Lt.W.ASHTON, M.C.   Wounded and at Duty.

OTHER RANKS.
Killed in Action:-   30
Wounded.   122
Missing.   5
Wounded & at Duty   5.

Great loss was inflicted on the enemy, whose dead were numerous all over the Battlefield. The captures amounted to 100 prisoners, 3 Guns, 3 Trench Mortars, 2 Anti-Tank Rifles and upwards of 60 M.Guns.

Battalion Headquarters moved forward to WHITE SPRING and Coys were re-organised on the Field.

At 5 p.m. the Battalion received orders to move into FOREST and billet there for the night, the 54th Inf.Brigade was to take over that portion of the front immediately N.E. of BOUSIES with the 6th Bn. Northamptonshire Regt, the 11th Bn.Royal Fusiliers being in Support and the 2nd Bn.Bedfordshire Regiment in Reserve. We were warned that we might be required to continue the attack in the morning and at 10 p.m. a message was received to the effect that the attack would be continued between 4 a.m. and 6 a.m. I immediately sent forward 2nd Lieut.W.TYSOE, D.S.O., with one officer per Company with instructions to reconnoitre the Ground and meet the Battalion at the EPINETTE Cross Roads on arrival.

PLAN.
At 12.30 a.m. a Conference took place at 54th Inf.Bde.Hd.Qrs at which we were given the role of passing through the right two Coys of 6th Northamptons on the first objective, viz., 200 yards N.E. of the REUMART FARM - LA FOURQUETTE Road and go on to the final objective - the line of the ENGLEFONTAINE - LANDRECIES Road.

Companies were detailed as follows:-
"A" (Right) and "D" (Left)., were to form up behind the 6th Northamptons and passing through them on their first objective seize the high ground in F.12 c.square 300 yards N.E. of the BROOK.

"B" Company (Right) and "C" Coy (Left) were to pass through the above two companies and fight their way on to the final objective.

Battalion Headquarters were to start at the Cemetery (BOUSIES) and move forward in rear of the Centre of the Battalion.

NARRATIVE.
The forming up was rendered exceedingly difficult by the enclosed nature of the Country and it was found necessary to form up in the road and move out in small columns. In spite of this and the short time at our disposal the Battalion was in position quarter of an hour before ZERO and duly moved off following the 6th Northamptons.

Continued

NARRATIVE (Continued).

On reaching the general line BOUSIES - WOOD FARM - F.23,Central - F.23.d.5/2, the Advance was held up by heavy Machine Gun fire from the High Ground in front and from our Right Flank. The latter especially was exceedingly uncomfortable and inflicted considerable casualties on our men.

Finding a large number of men on the line of the road running S.E. from BOUSIES WOOD FARM, consisting of men of all Units I ordered an officer of the 11th R.Fusrs, to collect all the men of his Battalion and take them on to his own post in the vicinity of BOUSIES WOOD FARM. A Platoon of the 6th Northamptons I sent to rejoin their own Company and then further thinned out the Line by ordering Lt.R.I.EDWARDS, M.C? who was in Command of "A" Company, to collect as many as possible of his Company and hold them in reserve in the ORCHARD about F.23.c.2.8.

"B" Company were left to hold the front line with advanced posts in the Valley about F.23.Central. "C" and "D" Coys were dug in protecting our right flank about F.29.a.7.5 to F.23.d.0.0.

In view of the heavy Machine Gun Fire which continued from our right flank I decided that further advance during daylight would be impossible without suffering heavy casualties.

I established Headquarters again at the Cemetery with advance report centre at F.23.c.3.5.

At about 9.15 a.m. a most regrettable incident occurred, an organised shoot by our heavy artillery falling short and causing two Companies to evacuate their positions, besides inflicting a number of casualties. This was duly reported but at 12.15 p.m. an exactly similar thing occurred again and again casualties were reported.

During the afternoon a fine exploit by Lt.HEDGES, 6th Bn.Northamptonshire Regt, who personally went forward with a Lewis Gun Section and cleared the Ridge on our immediate front enabled further operations to be undertaken. I had previously arranged with Lt.THOMPSON of the Tank Corps to work round our right flank at 4.30 p.m. with objective RENUARD FARM, taking on any enemy Machine Guns he encountered on the way and I now organised a joint attack on RENUARD FARM with one Platoon of the Queens and 2 Sections of the Bedfords, curiously enough, this attack coincided with that made by the Tank and the enemy was duly driven out of RENUARD FARM.

The way was now open for a further advance and accordingly at 6 p.m. I instructed Lt.R.I.EDWARDS, M.C., to feel his way forward and if possible make good our original objective, viz., the line of the ENGLEFONTAINE LANDRECIES Road.

I instructed 2nd Lt.I.L.WHITTINGHAM, Commanding "D" Coy, vice Capt. REISS (Wounded) to form a defensive flank by taking up a position facing S.E. between RENUARD FARM and the BROOK.

I moved "C" Company up in close support and kept "B" Company in reserve.

I sent 2nd Lieut.W.TYSOE,D.S.O. to form a report centre at RENUARD FARM and by 9.30 p.m. telephonic communication had been opened to here by Lieut.R.B.REDNALL, the Bn.Signalling Officer.

By 10 p.m. Lt.R.I.EDWARDS, M.C. reported his Company holding a position along the road running N.W. and S.E. in A.13.d.Square in touch with the E.Surreys on his right but a gap on his left. Contact had been obtained with the enemy at the road junction A.13.d.9½.05.

At 2 a.m. 25th October this line was handed over to the 10th Bn.Essex Regt.

REMARKS.

Although no opposition was encountered, I consider Lt.R.I.Edward's performance in moving forward his Company a distance of over a mile on a very dark night without loss of direction and again establishing contact with the enemy is worthy of considerable praise.

In conclusion, I wish to mention the excellent work done by the Tanks both on the 23rd and 24th October. They frequently appeared on the scene just when they were wanted and assisted the advance of the Infantry and they also displayed a fine spirit in returning to the fight in spite of having the majority of their crew wounded by Armour Piercing Bullets.

Lt.Colonel

29.10.18.   Commanding 2nd Battalion Bedfordshire Regiment.

2nd Bn.Bedfordshire Regt.
"   "   "   "
"   "   "   "
"   "   "   "

Casualties 24.10.15.

Capt.R.J.Reiss M.O. R.H.   wounded.
2nd Lieut.T.T.Hall.   wounded.
2nd Lieut.Dyson.   wounded.

Other Ranks

Killed   9
Wounded   39
Missing   4

Appendix II

Operation Order   No.35
By
Lt.Colonel A.E. Percival, D.S.O., M.C.
Commanding WIPE,

Ref.Map 57 B., N.E.

1. The Battalion will relieve the 8th E.Surrey Regt in the right Brigade Sub-Sector tomorrow and act as Brigade Reserve. Relief to be complete by 12 noon.

2. Companies will be disposed as arranged at Conference held this evening.

3. Guides will meet "A" Coy at F.29.c.2.7. and "B" and "C" Coys at L.5.c.5.4. at 0800.

4. Order of March.
"A" and "C" Coys will move off at 0715 and "D" and "B" Coys at 0730. Hd.Qrs will follow "B" Coy.
Coys will march by platoons at 200 yards interval.

5. Route as explained at Conference.

6. Headquarters will rendezvous at L.5.b.6.4., where Bn.Report Centre will open.

7. "D" Coy Cooker will proceed with "D" Coy.
"B" Coy Cooker and utensils for "A" and "C" and Hd.Qrs will be ready to move off when a guide returns for them.
A water cart will remain in EPINETTE.
2 Cooks per Coy will proceed to the line.

8. Completion of relief will be reported to E.Surreys Headquarters, ROBERSART.

9. O.C.'s "A" and "C" Coys will meet the Commanding Officer at L.5.b.6.4 at 1000.

10. Breakfast at 0600.

26.10.18   Sd. A.P.Methuen,   Lieutenant
                                       A/Adjutant, WIPE.

Appendix III

Operation Order No. 36
By
Major L.H. Keep, M.C.,
Commanding WIPE,
28.10.18.
-:-:-:-:-:-:-:-:-:-:-:-:-

1. WIPE (2.Bedf.R.) will releive JURU (11th R.Fusrs) in the right sector, tomorrow, 29th, inst.

2. DISPOSITIONS.
    "A" and "C" Coy front line.
    "A" Coy Right.   "C" Coy Left.
    "B" and "D" Coys Support Line.
    "B" Coy Right.   "D" Coy Left.
    as explained at Conference.

3. No body of troops to exceed a platoon.

4. Relief Complete will be sent by Coy Commanders.

5. "A" and "C" Coys rations will be cooked on arrival and taken up on the man.
    A Limber will report at 4.30 p.m. at Bn.Hd.Qrs to take dixies for all Coys and Hd.Qrs.

6. "D" Coy will take their Bivouac Sheets with them.

7. 6 Tins of Hot Tea will be available for each of the front line Coys at 2330.
    Coys will send their own carrying parties.

8. "A" Coy will hand in Bivouac Sheets to Bn.Hd.Qrs before leaving.

9. Receipted trench store lists will be rendered to Bn.Hd.Qrs by 1700.

10. "B" and "D" Coys will move off at 1615.
    "A" and "C" Coys at 1700.

28.10.18.   Sd. A.P.Methuen.   Lieutenant.
                                       A/Adjutant, WIPE.

1 DAJO
2 "A" Coy
3 "B" Coy
4 "C" Coy
5 "D" Coy
6 R.S.M.
7 MUSE
8 JURU

SECRET   Appendix IV.

2ND BN. BEDFORDSHIRE REGIMENT.   Operation Order. No.36.

September 27th 1918.

Ref. SHEETS. 62.c.N.E. and 57.c.S.E.

1. The Battalion will move tomorrow to an Area W. of EPEHY.

2. Starting Point - V.29.c.7.2.

3. Time - 3.45 a.m.

4. Order of March - Hd.Qrs, "A", "B", "C", & "D" Coys. Move by Companies at 2 minute intervals.

5. Dress - Battle Order, with blankets.

6. Route - Via Cross-country track to new billeting area about W.28 & 29 and E.4 and 5 squares. The exact position of new area will be notified later.

7. Lewis Gun Limbers will report to Companies at 7.0 p.m. today and will move with Companies tomorrow morning.

8. Cookers will proceed to the new area tonight and will have breakfast ready on arrival.

9. Officer's Valises, Mess boxes, etc. to be left behind will be dumped at Battalion Headquarters by 6.0 a.m. and will be collected by the Transport.

10. The Transport will move under Brigade arrangements at 11.0 a.m. tomorrow to the neighbourhood of SAULCOURT.

11. Company Commanders will reconnoitre the route to the new area this afternoon.

12. Movement in the new area must be reduced to a minimum. Cookers, water-carts etc, must be hidden as much as possible under banks and trees.

13. Orders as to Battle Surplus will be issued later.

14. ACKNOWLEDGE.

                                           Captain & A/Adjutant.
                                   2nd Battalion Bedfordshire Regiment.
Copy No. 1. C.O.
         2. O.C. "A" Coy.
         3. O.C. "B" Coy.
         4. O.C. "C" Coy.
         5. O.C. "D" Coy.
         6. Quartermaster.
         7. T.O.
         8. 54th Bde.
         9. R.S.M.
        10. War Diary.
        11. File.

6) All Stores will be taken over from
Northern [illeg] rebel camps and
distributed and so over to Br McG[?]

7) [illeg] of 1st [illeg] will be reported
by Coy Cmdrs [illeg]
[illeg] to [illeg] will be reported
by Coy Cmdr [illeg] [illeg] backwards.

8) Ration arrangements as yesterday.

9) Reconnaissance of [illeg] front
line to begin immediately

31/[?]   [signature] McM[illeg]
                                      Lieut
                          Sergt WIPE

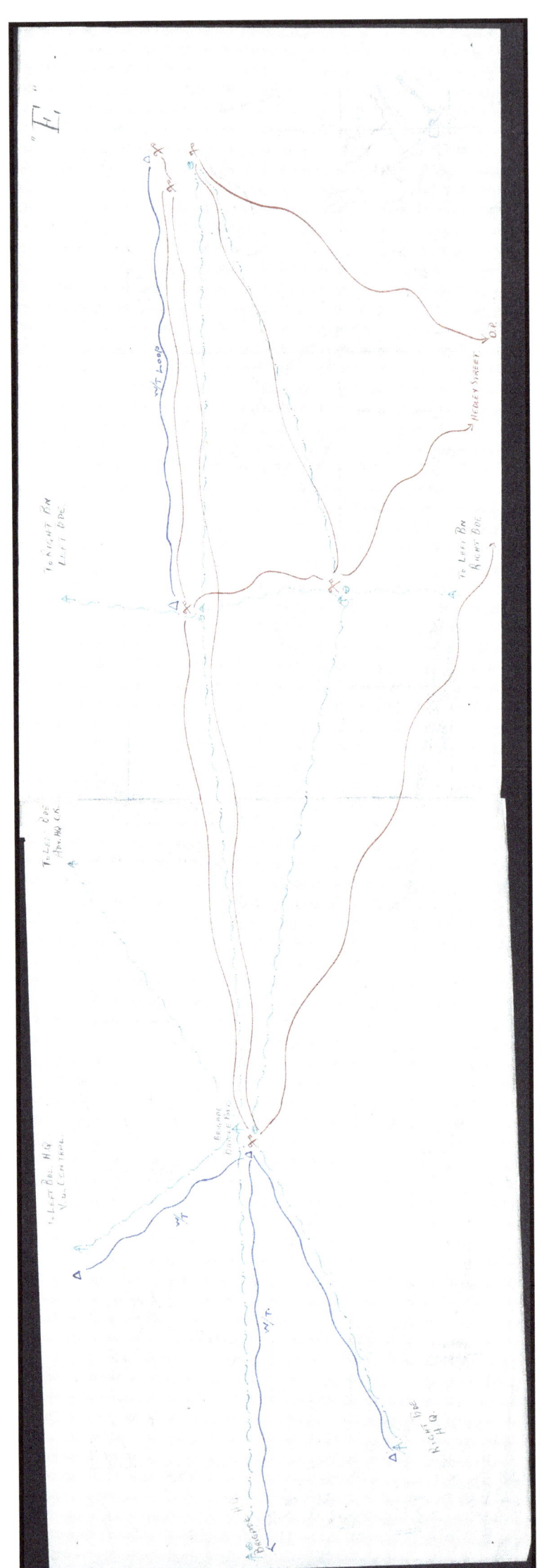

Appendix I

Following Congratulatory Wire received from General
Sir Ivor MAXSE.,(late Commander of 18th Corps) Inspector
General of Training, and General MORLAND, French Corps Comdr.

From. Gen. MORLAND.

" To 18th Division.   25.10.1918.

"Hearty congratulations to yourself, staff and all ranks
"on their great success of last two days which reflects the
"greatest credit on all concerned "

                             Sd.   MORLAND.

From Sir Ivor MAXSE.

Hearty congratulations to 18th Division on their splendid
fighting successes this week.

                             Sd.   MAXSE.

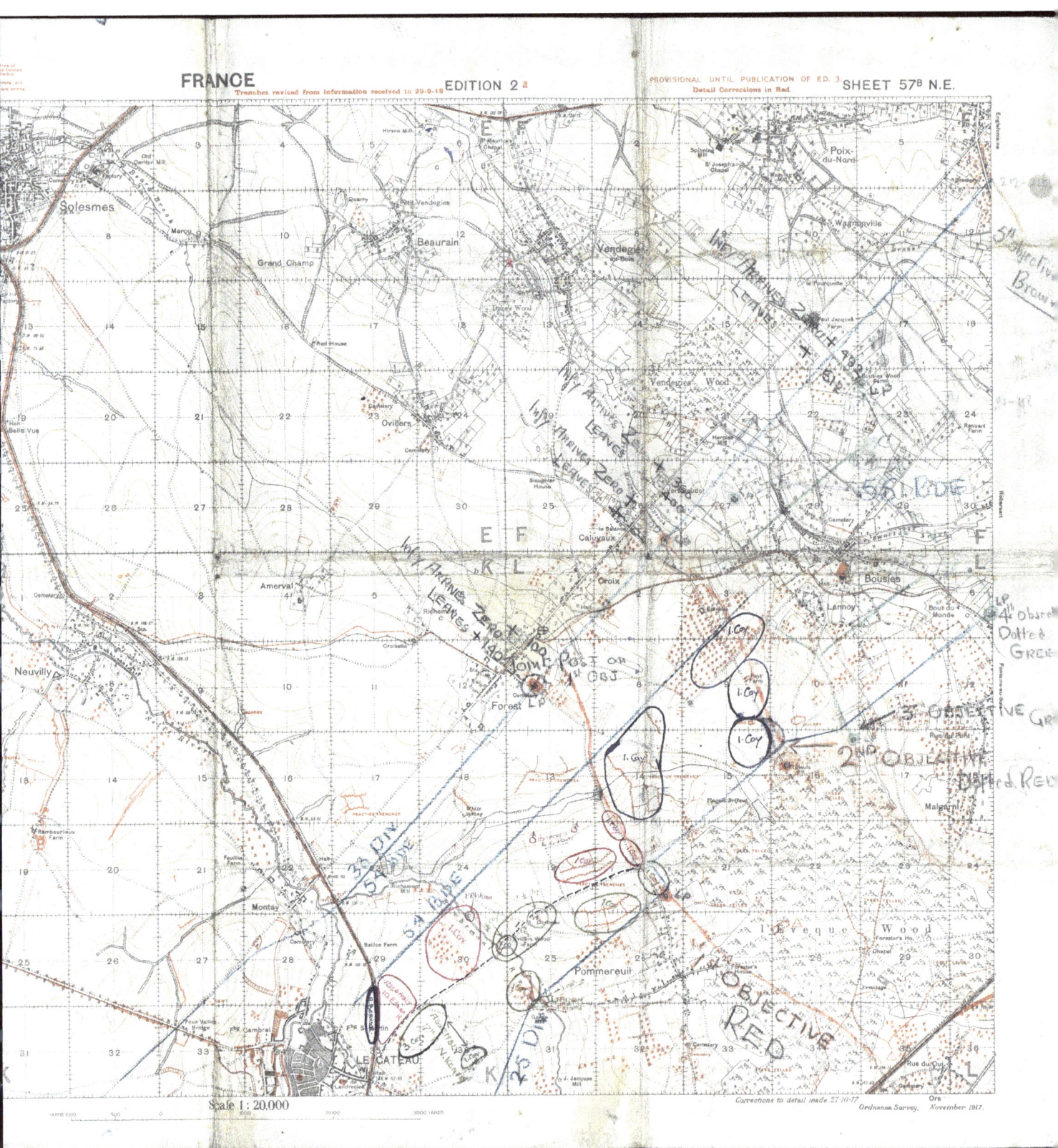

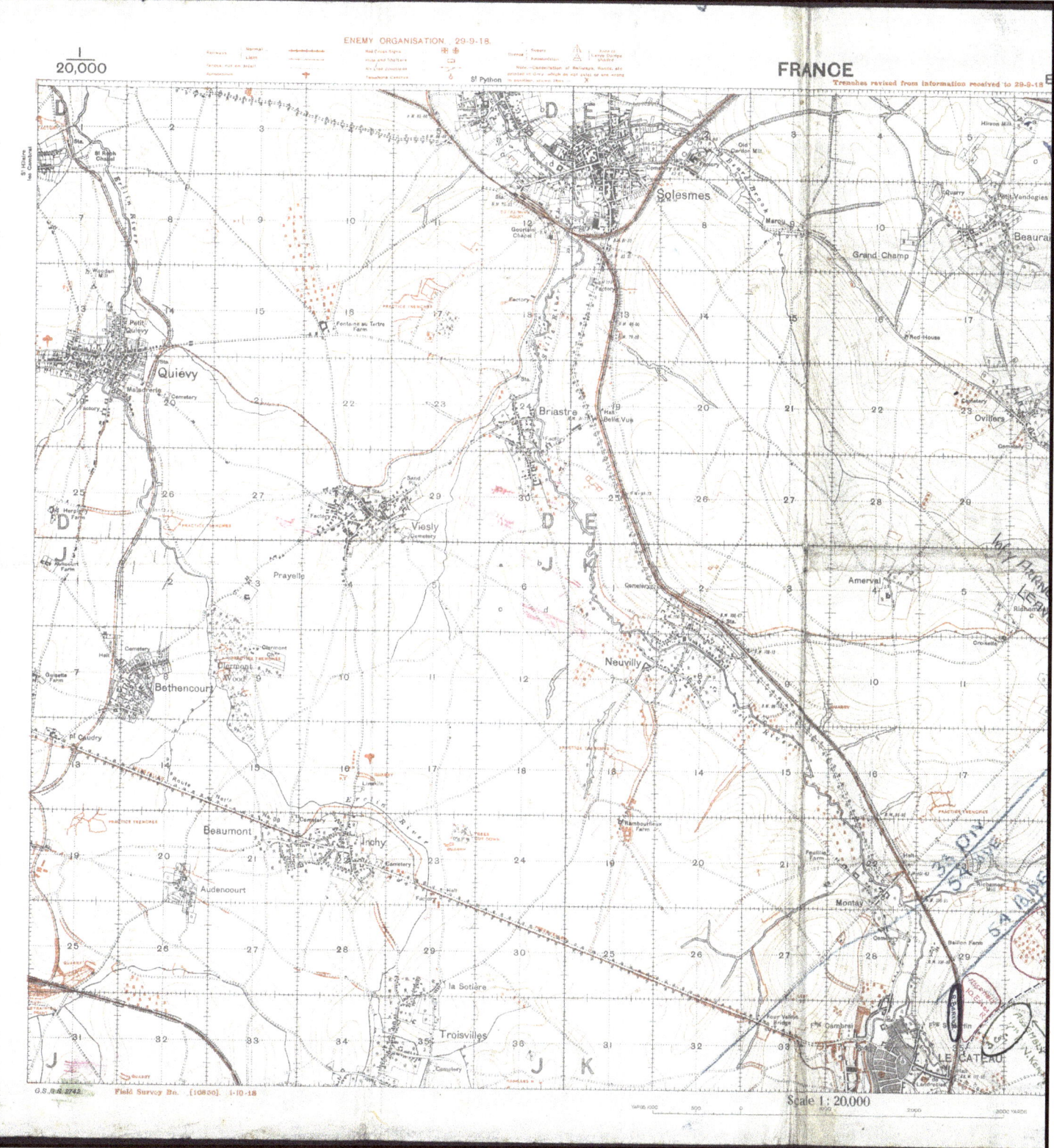

2nd Bedfordshire

54th Brigade

November 1915

WAR DIARY
or
INTELLIGENCE SUMMARY.

(Erase heading not required.)

Army Form C. 2118.

Instructions regarding War Diaries and Intelligence Summaries are contained in F.S. Regs., Part II. and the Staff Manual respectively. Title pages will be prepared in manuscript.

Place	Date	Hour	Summary of Events and Information	Remarks and references to Appendices
Field.	1st November.		Battalion were relieved by 11th Royal Fusiliers and took over dispositions in Reserve near BOUSIES. Lieut.P.W.Priestley., 2/Lieut.D.W.Wood., 2/Lieut. C.P.Marris. Joined Battalion. Casualties:- 1 O.R. Wounded.	(Appendix.1)
	2nd November.		On night 2/3rd inst. Battalion was resting at PREUX-AU-BOIS and was ordered to take part in attack against PREUX-AU-BOIS on 4.11.18. Casualties:- 2 O.R. Wounded. **AWARDS** Bar to the Military Medal 25466 L.C.J.Harris.MM.,17442 Pte.A.Goodliffe.DCM.MM.,15644 Pte.J.Jones.MM.,15364 L.C.A.Gurney.MM. Military Medal 266655 Pte.W.R.Furmston, 266188 Pte.F.Chapman., 16175 Cpl.S.Dines.,40129 Sgt,H.Kemble., 37824 Pte.T.W.Green., 31154 Pte.F.C.Jeffrey.15282 Sgt.B.Higgins, 9570 Cpl.A,Caress. 13042 Pte.C. Hare., 9523 Pte.F. Ludlow.	
	3rd November.		Battalion at BOUSIES.	
	4th November.		Operations against PREUX AU BOIS. Casualties:- 2/Lieut.S.A.G.Hill.Wounded.,2/Lieut.S.H.Abbott.Killed., 2/Lieut.W.Pennington.Wounded.,2/Lieut.W.Ashton MC. Wounded. Other Ranks:- 7 Killed.,34 Wounded.,3 Missing. Operations entirely successful.	(Appendix.II)
	5th November.		Battalion at PREUX-AU-BOIS resting.	
	6th November.		Battalion marched to LE CATEAU. Headquarters in RUE de LANDRECIES.	
	7th November.		Battalion at LE CATEAU Re-organising.	
	8th November.		Battalion at LE CATEAU Re-organising.	
	9th November.		Battalion at LE CATEAU training. Major.L.H.KEEP MC., awarded D.S.O.,Capt.G.E.GOTT. awarded M.C. No.49803 Pte.W.T.YORK. awarded Military Medal.	

Army Form C. 2118.

WAR DIARY
or
INTELLIGENCE SUMMARY.
(Erase heading not required.)

Instructions regarding War Diaries and Intelligence Summaries are contained in F. S. Regs., Part II. and the Staff Manual respectively. Title pages will be prepared in manuscript.

Place	Date	Hour	Summary of Events and Information	Remarks and references to Appendices
Field.	10th Novr.		Battalion at LE CATEAU. Church Parade.	
	11th	"	Battalion at LE CATEAU. Hostilities suspended at 11.0 a.m.	
	12th	"	Battalion at LE CATEAU Draft of 101 O.R. from Base. Lieut.A.J.Whitworth to Base unfit for Service at Front.	
	13th	"	Battalion marched to SERAIN. (Ref. Map SHEET 57.B).	Appendix III
	14th	"	Battalion at SERAIN training. Draft of 52 O.R. joined Battalion	
	15th	"	Battalion at SERAIN training. 10 O.R. from Base.	
	16th	"	Battalion at SERAIN training.	
	17th	"	Battalion at SERAIN. Church Parade, Thanksgiving Service.	
	18th	"	Battalion at SERAIN. 2 Companies on Salvage Work., 2 Companies Training. No.3/7668 Pte.G.H.Hutchings awarded Military Medal.	
	19th	"	Battalion at SERAIN on Salvage Work. Lieut.T.J.Pemberton joined Battalion from Base. 2/Lieut.G.W.Manners rejoined Battalion. Captain J.C.M.Ferguson died on 19.11.18. at ROUEN Military Hospital.	
	20th	"	Battalion at SERAIN on Salvage Work.	
	21st	"	Battalion at SERAIN on Salvage Work. 17 O.R. from Base.	
	22nd	"	Battalion at SERAIN on Salvage Work. 10 O.R. from Base.	
	23rd.	"	Battalion at SERAIN on Salvage Work.	

WAR DIARY
INTELLIGENCE SUMMARY.
(Erase heading not required.)

Army Form C. 2118.

Place	Date	Hour	Summary of Events and Information	Remarks and references to Appendices
Field.	24th Novr.	:	Battalion at SERAIN. Brigade Church Parade.	
	25th	:	Battalion at SERAIN. Salvage work and Training. 2/Lieut.G.Spence., 2/Lieut.C.H.C.Phillips., 2/Lieut.A.E.Thomas. Joined Battalion.	
	26th	:	Battalion at SERAIN. Salvage work & Training. 11 O.R.from Base.	
	27th	:	Battalion at SERAIN training.	
	28th	:	Battalion at SERAIN. Practise Divisional Review. Honours & Awards T/Lieut.R.T.Oldfield. MC. Bar to the M.C. T/Lieut.R.B.Rednall. The Military Cross. 2/Lieut.W. Pennington. The Military Cross. No.18258 Sgt.W.A.Ellis.DCM. Bar to D.C.M. The Distinguished Conduct Medal 50189 Pte.R.Jary., 42480 Pte.W.A.Suffolk., 17434 Sgt.C.H.Reynolds.,15459 Sgt.D.Collins., 26067 Cpl.J.Barford. 15364,L.C. A.Gurney.MM.	
	29th	:	Battalion at SERAIN training	
	30th	:	Battalion at SERAIN training. Honours & Awards The Military Medal 15789 Sgt.C.W.Reed., 19689 Pte.C.F.S.Hill., 18416 Pte.G.Stringer.,20341 Pte.R.H.Wiggins., 18931 L.C. E.F.Atkins.41650 Pte.W.W.Wale., 40811 CSM.O.H.Kirby., 21613 Cpl.W.Showell., 17572 Pte. W.Church. 202214 L.C.H.Murgatroyd.21053 Pte.A.W.Waters., 9707 Sgt.G.H.Rickard. 26061 Pte. G.Titmus. 266686 L.C.G.Humphreys. 10047 Cpl.R. Atkins., 10628 L.C. G.Berry. 42578 Pte. J.Griffin. "A"Company won Brigade Inter-Company Cross Country Race.	

A.C. Pennand.
Lieut.Colonel.
Commanding 2nd Battalion Bedfordshire Regiment.

ROBERSART

Intelligence Map.   Scale 1:20,000.

2nd Bn. Bedfordshire Regiment

Narrative of Operations 4.11.18 including attack on PREUX-AUX-BOIS.

Reference Sheet 57 A. N.W. 1/20,000.

PRELIMINARY. After holding the line in front of ROBERSART for 3 days the Battalion was relieved by the 11th Royal Fusiliers on the evening of the 1st November and went into Support on the S.E. outskirts of BOUSIES.

The general plan of attack had been explained to O.C.Battalions at a Brigade Conference held on the 31st October and reconnaissances of the ground over which the operations were to take place were carried out on the 1st November and succeeding days.

The PLAN. The 54th Brigade in conjunction with the 53rd Infantry Brigade on the left and 150th Infantry Brigade on the Right, was to take part on the 4th November in an attack on a wide front on the German positions. Objective of the 54th Brigade was PREUX-AUX-BOIS and the orchards to the N. of its as far as the edge of the FORET de MORMAL.

6th Northamptonshire Regt. were to advance at Zero and capture the orchards in A.14.a & b. and A.15.a. squares; 2nd Bedfordshire Regt, forming up in the orchards in A.13.b.square were to follow the 6th Northamptons and, facing right, were to attack PREUX- AUX-BOIS and orchards in the vicinity from the North in conjunction with one Company of 11th Royal Fusiliers on the Right and one Company of 6th Northamptons on the left.

11th Royal Fusiliers (less 1 Company) were to hold existing front line West of PREUX and make a demonstration.

Companies were allotted roles as under:-
"C" Coy.(Right) and "A" Coy (Left) were to lead the attack. "C" Coy being responsible for the orchards in A.14.d. and A.20.b. squares between the main street on the East and the stream on the West, and "A" Coy. being responsible for both houses on both sides of the street running North and South from A.15.a.0.7. to A.21.a.0.4.

About the line running East and West through A.21.a.0.4. "D" Company (Right) and "B" Coy. (Left) were to pass through the above two Companies and push on to the final objective A.20.d.2.5. to A.21.c.5.7., where liaison was to be made with the 2nd Battalion Royal Munster Fusiliers.

Two Tanks were allotted to the Battalion, one of which was to proceed with the Right two Companies and the other with the Left 2 Companies.

The APPROACH MARCH. The march to the Assembly position on account of the darkness of the night and the advisability of avoiding the roads which were kept under constant bursts of Machine Gun fire, was realised to be a matter of some difficulty and every precaution was therefore taken to prevent the Platoons losing the way. In addition to Platoon representatives being taken over the ground on the preceding day, the Battalion Scouts under Lieut.A.W.G.Smith, were employed in marking out the route by means of bicycle lamps and white tape.

At 2345 hours the Companies commenced to move up and thanks to the above precautions the approach march was carried out without difficulty with the loss of 1 N.C.O.killed.

Battalion Headquarters moved forward to the SUNKEN Road A.13.b.8.5.

THE ATTACK. At 0615 the barrage opened and at 0650 the Companies commenced to move forward in rear of the 6th Northamptonshire Regt, who made an excellent and spirited attack and cleared the whole of the area over which the Battalion had to advance.

Companies duly reached the forming up position and lined up just North of the brook in A.14.d.square waiting for the enfilade barrage to start at 0807. A very heavy enfilade shrapnel barrage, with 4.5.howitzers beyond, came down on the line of the brook and after a pause of 4 minutes commenced to move South at the rate of 100 yards in 5 minutes.

"C" Company on the Right, under command of Captain R.L.V.Ponke MC, closely followed by "D" Company, commanded by 2/Lieut.W.Pennington, at once commenced to make good progress, though a number of the

contd.

enemy were encountered in the orchards. The latter both fighting well, were taken in flank and quickly overcome thanks to the splendid leading of the Officers and N.C.Os of "C" and "D" Coys, many small local attacks and enveloping movements being organised on the spur of the moment and successfully carried out.

"C" Company arrived on their objective shortly after scheduled time and leaving garrisons at important points pushed on into the Village in Support of "D" Company. Here a large number of the enemy were encountered in the streets and the cellars and taken prisoners and at about 0930 "D" Company had reached their final objective and got into touch with the 2nd Bn.Royal Munster Fusiliers.

I consider the success of "D" and "D" Companies was largely due to the splendid leading of the Officers, Captain.R.L.V. Donke. MC, 2/Lieut T.F.Vaughan and 2/Lieut.W.Ashton MC (Wounded) ("C" Company) and 2/Lieut W.Pennington (Wounded) & 2/Lieut.I.L.Whittingham ("D" Company). These Officers, well backed up by their N.C.Os, led their Companies forward in spite of the attack being held up on both flanks and by their action enables the rest of the attack to go on.

On the left "A" Company command by Lieut.A.F.Aldridge, had almost immediately been held up by Machine Gun Fire from the road junction A.15.c.0.5., causing them to lose the barrage. Two attempts were made by a Tank to deal with this strong point, but without success.

Elements of the two right Platoons of "A" Company however well led by Lieut. W.J.Holbrook, MC, were able to work round the West of the strong point and attacked the enemy in the Cemetery at A.14.d.9.4. which was cleared after a spirited struggle.

This opened the way for the Right two Platoons of "B" Company under 2/Lieut.H.B.Lang to move forward and clear the main street as far as the road junction A.21.c.3.8. An isolated Machine Gun Nest which was harrasing troops in the Village from about A.21.a.5.0. was engaged and finally mopped up by a party led by 2/Lieut.H.B.Lang.

Meanwhile the Left two Platoons of "A" Company under Lieut. A.F. Aldridge and the Left two Platoons of "B" Company under 2/Lieut.S.W. Goble MC. had worked their way round the East of the Strong point at A.15.c.0.5. and were clearing the houses along the side of the lane running S.E. and N.W. in A.15.c.square. The enemy in the Strong point at A.15.c.0.5. seeing themselves outflanked and being attacked from the rear, now gave in.

It was found on examination that the Machine Gun had been firing through a hole in the wall of a house well camouflaged.

At 1100 Lieut.A.W.G.Smith, the Intelligence Officer, was sent forward and established a forward report centre at PREUX-AUX-BOIS and by 12 noon all the village was clear and the way was opens for other troops to pass through.

Battalion Headquarters moved forward to A.20.b.95.65 and Companies were reorganised and billeted in PREUX.

The battalion's Casualties were:-

Officers.

2/Lieut S.H. Abbott. Killed.
2/Lieut.W. Ashton.MC. Wounded.
2/Lieut.W. Pennington.Wounded.
2/Lieut.S.A.G.Hill. Wounded.

Other Ranks.

& 7 Killed.
33 Wounded.
3 Missing.

Captures included 300 prisoners, 20 Machine Guns, 3 heavy Trench Mortars and 1 Anti-Tank Rifle, besides much other material.

Prisoners must of whom were Jaegers stated that practically the whole of the defence was concentrated on the PREUX line; this was borne out by subsequent events as directly the way was clear to the Forest, the troops passed through and met with practically no resistance.

1400 Civilians were liberated in PREUX.

contd.

CONCLUSION:- The success of the attack and the small number of
casualties suffered appears to have been due firstly to the
well conceived plan of taking the village from the North.
Most of the enemy Machine Gun positions were sited in hedges
facing West and by attacking them in flank it was possible
to work along the hedges and get close to them before being seen.
Secondly I consider the success to have been due to the adoption
of principles recently taught in training, namely, the value of
local flanking movements when dealing with enemy Machine Guns.
The thick hedges and enclosed nature of the country was
peculiarly adapted to these tactics.

Thirdly to the dash and drive and quickness to take advantage
of an opening shown by all ranks.

The tanks were useful in breaking down hedges but were not
on this occasion of much assistance in helping the advance as one
broke down and two others were put out of action before they had
gone very far.

All ranks are unanimous in their praise of the Barrage,
which was both thick and accurate.

Bill-hooks were carried and were exceedingly useful in getting
through the thick hedges.

Casualties were saved by a careful choice of the assembly
position which was just clear of the enemy barrage line.

The Medical Officer established an Aid Post near the front
line where he worked unceasingly all morning attending to casualties
of all units of the Division without assistance

7.11.1918.   Commanding 2nd Bn, Bedfordshire Regiment.   Lt.Colonel

Copiss to:-
    C.O. (2)
    Maj.L.H.Keep, M.C.
    O.C. each Coy
    54tht Brigade.
    War Diary (2)
    Lt.A.P.Methuen.
    Spare copies (2)
    Adjutant.

"A" Form
MESSAGES AND SIGNALS.

Army Form C. 2121
(in pads of 100.)

Reference —
Sheets 57A & B —

Appendix

TO All Companies.
Transport Officer.
Sergt. Cobbold.

Day of Month: 6th.

AAA

1. The Battalion will move to LE CATEAU by route march to-day.
2. Starting point: Crossroads A.20.d.50.05.
3. Time: 1155
4. Order of March: H.Q. D. C. B. A.
5. March by Companies at 200yds distance.
6. Dress: Battle Order. Blankets rolled round the haversack. Steel Helmets worn.
7. Tools. Company Commanders will ensure that all picks & shovels are taken back. They will be carried on the men. Billhooks will be put on the L.G. limbers.
8. Route: A.25.b.4.0 — BOUSIES — L.2 — FOREST — K.18.b.0.0 —

"A" Form
MESSAGES AND SIGNALS.

Army Form C. 2121 (in pads of 100.)

K.29.b+c

9. Company L.G. limbers will march with the companies + will be under the orders of O.C. Companies.

10. Guides will meet Companies on arrival at K.35.a.2.4.

11. Dinners will be ready on arrival.

12. O.C. Companies will ensure that the men parade as clean as possible & that strict march discipline is maintained during the march.

13. ACKNOWLEDGE.

H. Guy Phillips
Capt. & Adjt.

SECRET.

54th Infantry Brigade.
ADMINISTRATIVE INSTRUCTIONS issued with ORDER No. 200.

Ref. Map:
Sheet FOREST
1/20,000.
                                                              2nd November, 1918.

1. **1st LINE TRANSPORT.**

   If situation permits, it is hoped to move 1st Line Transport to an area in vicinity of BOUSIES on Z "Z" Day.

   (a) "A" Echelon (less Pack Train detailed below) organised as per my S.C.304 of 16/10/18, will stand to in present Transport Lines from Z plus 4 hours, ready to move at 1 hour's notice.

   (b) A Pack Train, composed as under, under orders of Lieut. Stanbury, Transport Officer, 6th Northamptonshire Regt., with one N.C.O. to be detailed by 2nd Bedfordshire Regt., will report at Bde. H.Q. F.28.c.0.0. at Zero plus 3 hours. :-

      15 Packs (5 per Battalion) complete with loads (S.A.A. Bandolier).
      Limber No. 5. of 2nd Bedfordshire Regt.   )
      Limber No. 6. of 6th Northamptonshire Regt.) loaded.

   The days rations and forage to be carried.

   (c) "B" Echelon and Q.M.Stores will be prepared to move at 2 hours' notice from Zero plus 5 hours.

   Baggage waggons will report to units tomorrow, 3rd instant.

   In the event of supplies not being delivered by the time "B" Echelon moves off, guides will be left to bring wagons on to new location.
   Supply Wagons will not return until definite location of new lines is determined.

2. **SUPPLIES.**

   On and from 4th instant, supplies will be delivered to units by Train Transport.

   Rations on Z/Z plus 1 night will be delivered in usual manner, unless otherwise ordered. Battalion Advanced H.Q. will notify Brigade Rear H.Q. time at which rations should reach Brigade Advanced H.Q., and will arrange for guides to be there by that time.

3. **COMFORTS.**

   Additional issues of Rum, Oxo or Pea Soup will be made to troops in line.

   The travelling Soup Kitchen is available; Battalions will notify Brigade Rear H.Q. by 6 p.m., 3rd instant, if they desire to make use of same.

P.T.O.

4. AMMUNITION.

The following dumps have been formed:-

(a) At A.19.b.7.3. (in Sunken Road), containing:-

    S.A.A.   Bandolier   6 boxes.
            Bundle packed. 6 "

    Grenades No. 23.   350 rounds.
            No. 36.   350 "

    V.P.A.   White.   2 boxes.
           Red.   1 box.
           Green.   1 "

This Dump is exclusively for use of Battalion operating in that area.

(b) Brigade Main Dump, RODERSART (A.25.b.2.1.), containing:-

    S.A.A.   Bandolier   50 boxes.
           Bundle packed. 30 boxes.

    Lewis Gun Drums filled. 300.

    Grenades. No. 23.   756 rounds.
             No. 36.   756 "

    T.M.C.   360 rounds.

    V.P.A   White.   6 boxes.
          Red.   2 "
          Green.   2 "

    Water.   60 tins.

(c) Each fighting Tank attached to this Brigade will carry 5 boxes S.A.A. (Bandolier), which will be available if required.

Units will, as usual, demand on Brigade Headquarters.
An Orderly from No. 3. Section, D.A.C., is being attached to Brigade Transport Officer to connect with D.A.C.

5. R.E. DUMPS.

    Corps Dump.   P.17.a.9.4.
    Divisional Dump.   K.29.Central.

Units will demand as usual on Brigade Headquarters.

6. ROADS.

Practically every road and lane in Divisional areais being cleared by either the Field Companies or 8th Royal Sussex Pioneers.

The best map shewing all roads is Intelligence Map "C".

Before Transport has to proceed, it is hoped to have all cross roads marked with notice boards.

7. **BATHS.**

As soon as the situation permits, Spray Baths will be erected at the Factory, BOUSIES. Application for same to be made to Brigade Rear H.Q.

8. **SURPLUS KIT DUMP.**

A Dump for Blankets, Greatcoats, etc., is being formed in BOUSIES, No. 46. Billet, F.28.c.2.0. All surplus kit must be dumped by midnight, 3rd instant, so that all Battalion Stores, etc., may be carried in one journey when "B" Echelon is ordered forward. On no account may two journeys be made by transport. Brigade Transport Officer will ensure that this order is carried out.

Each Battalion will arrange for one man to be at this dump to act as guard, except in case of 2nd Belfordshire Regt., who will detail a N.C.O.

9. **CASUALTIES.**

New phase for estimated casualties commenced 0001, 1st instant.

Estimated Casualty Reports must not be confused with Accurate Casualty Reports, which will be rendered in the usual manner. Attention is directed to Fourth Army "A" Notes Part I. Estimated Reports should only be sent in after 50 or more O.R. Casualties have been sustained.

It is essential that all officer casualties be wired at earliest possible moment. Date of casualty must be stated.

10. **PROVOST ARRANGEMENTS.**

    Corps Prisoners of War Cage   -   REUMONT.
    Divisional Prisoners of War Cage -   Advanced Divisional Headquarters.

    Prisoners will be taken over by D.A.P.M. at Brigade Headquarters.

    Stragglers Posts :   L.4.c.4.9.   L.3.b.8.9.

    Stragglers Collecting Post: Advanced Divisional Headquarters.

11. **MEDICAL ARRANGEMENTS.**

(a) Officer Commanding, 55th Field Ambulance, is in charge of Advanced Evacuation. Headquarters : BOUSIES L.3.b.8.8.
He will have at his disposal the Bearer Divisions, Horsed Ambulances, Motor Ambulances and Wheeled Stretcher Carriers of 54th and 56th Field Ambulances.

(b) Officer Commanding, 56th Field Ambulance, will be in charge of Divisional Sick Station, MAUROIS.

(c) Regimental Aid Posts will be selected by Battalions concerned.

    Ford Car Loading Post   -   F.29.c.4.4.

    Walking Wounded Collecting Post.)   Near Station, BOUSIES,
    Advanced Dressing Station.   )   L.3.b.8.8.

    Corps Main Dressing Station.)   Le CATEAU, K.34.a.8.3.
    Corps Walking Wounded Post.)

(d) Method of evacuation. Lying Cases by hand carriage and wheeled stretchers to Ford Car Post, thence by Cars to Advanced Dressing Station. Walking Wounded will be directed through ROBERSART to Advanced Dressing Station, horsed Ambulances will meet them as far forward as possible.
It is proposed to push Ford Cars as far forward as possible.

P.T.O.

4.

12. **BURIAL PARTY.**

Battalions will be prepared to detail burial party as under to work under Lieut. A. E. DOWLEY, Divisional Burial Officer.

	N.C.Os.	Men.
11th Royal Fusiliers.	1	6
2nd Bedfordshire Regt.	1	6
6th Northamptonshire Regt.	-	6

13. **HEADQUARTERS.**

Brigade Rear Headquarters will move to present Advanced Brigade Headquarters BOUSIES, F.28.c.0.0.) at 1800 hours "Y" Day.

                                                             Beasley
                                                       Captain,
                                                 A/Staff Captain,
                                                 54th Inf. Bde.

Distribution   All Recipients O/200
                   plus :-
                      All Battalions (Rear).
                      Lieut Stanbury 6th North'n R.

SECRET

Appendix III

2nd Battalion Bedfordshire Regiment Order No.41.

Reference Map. SHEET. 57.B.   12th November 1918.

1. The Battalion will march to SERAIN tomorrow, November 13th.

2. Starting Point - Bridge K.34.b.0.1.

3. Time - 0740.

4. Route.- K.33.a.4.6. - HARETZ - W.21.d.7.9.

5. Order of March - Drums, Hd.Qrs. "A","B","C" & "D" Coys.

6. Distance between Companies - 100 yards.

7. Dress - Fighting Order. Caps will be worn - Steel helmets on back of the haversack, blankets rolled round the haversack and waterproof sheets on the belt. Rifle covers will not be on the rifles unless it is wet.

8. Reveille will be at 0600. Breakfast will be at 0630. Dinners on arrival.

9. Packs will be dumped by Companies and Headquarters at Quartermaster Stores by 0630. They will contain Great Coat and Jerkin and must be clearly marked on the back with number name and Company.
Drummers Blankets will be dumped at the same place and time.
Officers valises will be dumped at the Quartermaster Stores by 0730.

10. Transport.(1) A.Echelon will accompany the Battalion.
(2) All A Echelon will be across the Bridge at K.34.b.0.1. before 0730, and will await the arrival of the Battalion there.
(3) Lewis Gun Limbers will march with Companies, one Gun will be mounted on each Lewis Gun Limber and a Lewis Gunner will accompany the Limber.
(4) The remainder of A Echelon will march 100 yards in rear of "D" Coy.
(5) B.Echelon will march under the Brigade Transport Officer passing the Starting Point at 0835.
(6) Supply wagons will move under orders of O.C. No.3.Coy.Divisional Train.
(7) Officer's Chargers will report at Battalion and Company Hd.Qrs at 0725.

11. Advance Party. One N.C.O. per Company and Battalion Hd.Qrs will report to 2/Lieut.W.Tysoe.DSO. at Headquarter Mess at 0700. They will bring bicycles with them and will be in possession of accurate parade states.

12. ACKNOWLEDGE.

                                    sgd. H.SEYS-PHILLIPS. Captain.
                        Adjutant, 2nd Bn. Bedfordshire Regiment.

Copies to:-
(1) Commanding Officer.
(2) O.C."A" Coy.
(3) O.C."B" Coy.
(4) O.C."C" Coy.
(5) O.C."D" Coy.
(6) Quartermaster.
(7) Transport Officer.
(8) R.S.M.
(9) 2/Lt.W.Tysoe.DSO.
(10) & (11) War Diary.
(12) Adjutant.
(13) 54th Bde.

18th Division No.G. 375

The following letter addressed to
Major-General Lee has been received.

H.Q. Fourth Army.
23rd November, 1918.

My dear Lee,

I have not had time to come and see you, and therefore write these few lines to express to you, and to all ranks of the 18th Division, my warmest thanks for the splendid work that has been done by the Division, not only during these 100 days which have won us the war, but from March 1918 onwards.

The fine spirit of discipline and fighting energy which had characterised the 18th Division throughout these operations has filled me with admiration, and I offer to all ranks my warmest thanks for their gallantry and skill in so many hard-fought battles.

I specially call to mind the strenuous times before GENTELLES and CACHY, the taking of ALBERT and MEAULTE, the capture of BERNAFAY and TRONES Woods, the forcing of the TORTILLE River, the battles around and beyond RONSSOY and finally the attacks on BOUSIES, HECQ, and the FORET DE MORMAL.

It is, indeed, a record that every Officer, N.C.O. and man, has a right to be proud of, and I very much regret that you are not marching to the frontier with the Fourth Army.

The very best of luck to you all and again a thousand thanks for the brilliant part which the Division has played in these battles of the 100 days.

Yours sincerely,

(sgd) H. RAWLINSON.

Major-General R.P.LEE, C.B.
Comdg. 18th Division.

The following reply has been sent.

25th November, 1918.

My dear General,

All ranks of the 18th Division join in thanking you for your generous appreciation of the part they have played in the closing phase of this Great War.
The Division has done much of its fighting in the Fourth Army, commencing with the SOMME Battles in 1916 and ending so gloriously in the 100 days of victory, and will ever be grateful to you for your counsel and leadership.
Many of us still hope to rejoin your Army in Rhineland.

Yours sincerely,

(sgd) R.P.LEE.

General Sir H.S.RAWLINSON, Bart, G.C.V.O., K.C.B., K.C.M.G.
Commanding Fourth Army.

Army Form C. 2118.

WAR DIARY
or
INTELLIGENCE SUMMARY.
(Erase heading not required.)

Instructions regarding War Diaries and Intelligence Summaries are contained in F. S. Regs., Part II. and the Staff Manual respectively. Title pages will be prepared in manuscript.

Place	Date	Hour	Summary of Events and Information	Remarks and references to Appendices
In Field.	Dec.1st.		Battalion at SERAIN. Brigade Church Parade. 5 O.R. rejoined Battalion from Base.	
	Dec.2nd.		Battalion at SERAIN. Review of Division by Major Gen. R.P.Lee,C.B. Commanding 18th Division at U.15.square. Reference Map France 57.B. 1/40000. 6 O.R. rejoined Battalion from Base.	
	Dec.3rd.		Battalion at Training. 4 O.R. rejoined Battalion from Base.	
	Dec.4th.		Battalion at SERAIN. His Majesty the King visited SERAIN. The Battalion lined the roads and the King walked through the Ranks. T/Lieut.R.T.Oldfield.MC. to be Acting Captain from 19.10.18. Lieut.A.P.Methuen to be Acting Captain from 28.10.18.	
	Dec.5th.		Battalion at SERAIN. 1 Company on Salvage. Remainder Training. 2/Lieut. L.S.Rowe joined Battalion. 12 O.R. joined from Base. No.17572 L.Cpl. W.Church. MM. awarded Bar to M.M. 8 O.R. proceeded to England for 12 months rest under Substitution scheme.	
	Dec.6th.		Battalion at SERAIN. Companies at Training.	
	" 7th.		Battalion at SERAIN training. Lieut.W.Dayrell-Steyning., 2/Lt.P.H.Luntley., 2/Lt.J.H.Allpress, joined Battalion	
	8th.		Battalion at SERAIN. Brigade Church Parade. 7 O.R. rejoined from Base.	
	9th		Battalion at SERAIN. Salvage work & training. Honours & Awards. T.G.Lt. R.L.V.Doake.MC. Awarded D.S.O. Military Cross 2/Lt.H.B.Lang., 2/Lt.W.Tysoe.DSO., Lieut.D.F.Howard., Lieut.H.D.Chester., 2/Lt.I.I.Whittingham., Lieut.A.W.G.Smith., Captain J.Thompson. (R.A.M.C.) attached. D.C.M.:-15237 Sgt.C.W.Duhler., 18817 Sgt.D.Tynn.MM., 21583 Pte.F.Fluke.,2930 CSM.W.Clarke., 14854 Sgt.J.R.Robertson.,219336 Pte.J.Lardner.	

Army Form C. 2118.

WAR DIARY
or
INTELLIGENCE SUMMARY.
(Erase heading not required.)

Instructions regarding War Diaries and Intelligence Summaries are contained in F.S. Regs., Part II. and the Staff Manual respectively. Title pages will be prepared in manuscript.

Place	Date	Hour	Summary of Events and Information	Remarks and references to Appendices
In Field.	Dec.10th		Battalion at SERAIN, training. 8 O.R. from Base. Captain.R.I.Edwards. MC. to Adjutants School, Cambridge.	
	11th.		Battalion at SERAIN, training. 5 O.R. (Coalminers) despatched to England.	
	12th.		Battalion at SERAIN, training. Captain.H.C.Browning.MC. rejoined Battalion.	
	13th.		Battalion at SERAIN. Battalion Parade for Reception of Colours. Battalion marched to SELVIGNY.	
	14th.		Battalion at SELVIGNY. Employed at improving Billets. Captain. H.Driver. DSO. MC. rejoined Battalion. 11 O.R. rejoined from Base. Battalion H.Qrs played 54th Field Ambulance at Football in final for Inter-Company Bde. Football Cup & lost 2 - 1.	
	15th.		Battalion at SELVIGNY. - Brigade Church Parade.	
	16th.		Battalion at SELVIGNY. - Salvage Work.	
	17th.		Battalion at SELVIGNY. - Salvage work.	
	18th.		Battalion at SELVIGNY. - Salvage work in LESDAINS.	
	19th.		Battalion at SELVIGNY. - Bathing.	
	20th.		Battalion at SELVIGNY. - Salvage work in LESDAINS.	
	21st.		Battalion at SELVIGNY. - Kit Inspection. Rugby Football Match.- 46th Div v 18th Div. 46th Div winning by 6 points to 3.	
	22nd.		Battalion at SELVIGNY. - Brigade Church Parade. HONOURS & AWARDS:- . MILITARY MEDAL 10833 L.C.P.Whitworth, 41369 Pte.A.Moore., 28403 Pte.F.Harpur., 14258 Pte.J.C.Nymett. 4/4964 : J.Bennett., 9604 : F.Myles., 31350 : W.J.Carter., 3/7474 Pte.P.Clarke., 18250 Sgt.W.G.Baldwin., 16922 Pte.A.Knight.17674 : J.Corkett (attd 54th T.M.B)	

Army Form C. 2118.

WAR DIARY
or
INTELLIGENCE SUMMARY.
(Erase heading not required.)

Instructions regarding War Diaries and Intelligence Summaries are contained in F. S. Regs., Part II. and the Staff Manual respectively. Title pages will be prepared in manuscript.

Place	Date	Hour	Summary of Events and Information	Remarks and references to Appendices
In Field	Dec.23rd.		Battalion at SELVIGNY. Xmas Holiday. 6 O.R. rejoined from Base.	
	Dec.24th.		Battalion at SELVIGNY. Xmas Holiday.	
	Dec.25th.		Battalion at SELVIGNY. Xmas Holiday. Brigade Church Parade.	
	Dec.26th.		Battalion at SELVIGNY. Xmas Holiday	
	Dec.27th.		Battalion at SELVIGNY. Salvage work continued in LESDAINS Area.	
	Dec.28th.		Battalion at SELVIGNY. Parades under Company arrangements.	
	Dec.29th.		Battalion at SELVIGNY. Brigade Church Parade. Lt.R.B.Rednall,MC.appointed Salvage officer	
	Dec.30th.		Battalion at SELVIGNY. Salvage work in LESDAINS Area.	
	Dec.31st.		Battalion at SELVIGNY. Bathing. MENTIONED IN DESPATCHES. Extract from the Times dated 27th December 1918. Lt.Colonel.A.E.Percival.DSO.,MC. Lieut.(A/Major) J.T.Coe. Attd. 2/23rd.London Regt, Quartermaster & Major.H.Cressingham. DSO.,DCM. Lieut.(A/Major) A.Grover. DSO., MC. Attd 2/4th London Regt. T/2nd Lieut.W.Tysoe. DSO.,MC. Captain (A/Lt.Col.) R.O.Wynne. DSO. No.9509 Sgt.J.Allen.MM., 9246 Sgt.F.Coxall., 18076 Pte.H.G.Pepper., 43592 Pte.G.M.Sparkes., No.21055 Cpl.T.J.Williams MM. (attd.89th.T.M.B).	
	6.1.19.			

V.N.D.Rup
Major.
Commanding 2nd Bn. Bedfordshire Regiment

Army Form C. 2118.

WAR DIARY
or
INTELLIGENCE SUMMARY.

(Erase heading not required.)

Instructions regarding War Diaries and Intelligence Summaries are contained in F.S. Regs., Part II. and the Staff Manual respectively. Title pages will be prepared in manuscript.

Place	Date	Hour	Summary of Events and Information	Remarks and references to Appendices
Field.	1st to 31st January.		THE BATTALION WERE BILLETED AT SELVIGNY FROM 1ST TO 31ST JANUARY 1919.	

INCREASE.

Lieutenant. D.F.HOWARD. MC. rejoined Battalion from 54th Bde. Intelligence Officer and taken on strength 1.1.19.

DECREASE.

Lieut. T.J.Pemberton, appointed 54th Brigade Intelligence Officer and Struck off Strength. During January the following Officers and 163 Other Ranks were Demobilized:-

2/Lieut. I.L.Whittingham. MC. Demobilized 1.1.19.
Lieut. P.W.Priestley. " 17.1.19.
2/Lieut. C.J.Sturges. " 20.1.19.
Lieut. G.W.Manners. " 24.1.19.
2/Lieut. C.L.Tooley. " 27.1.19.

HONOURS & AWARDS

Lt. Colonel. A.E. Percival. DSO., MC. - Mentioned in Despatches 27.12.18.
No. 9707 Sergeant. G.H. Rickard. MM.   - Awarded Distinguished Conduct Medal. (B.o.2.1.19)
Capt.(A/Lt.Col) A.E.Percival.DSO.MC.   - To Be Brevet Major. Gazette dt.1.1.19.
9000 C/QMS. A.Sumner. Awarded D.C.M.   - Gazette dated 2.1.19.
20783 Cpl. T.Adams, awarded Belgian Decoration Militaire 26.1.19.
7091 Supt.Clk. J.A.Shrives   - Awarded Meritorious Service Medal. 18.1.19.
17047 QMS. E.P.Kerrison.DCM.   -   "   "   "
9283 Pnr.Sgt. J.Wheeler.MM.   -   "   "   "
43580 L/C. T. Holt.   -   "   "   "
Lt.Colonel.A.E. Percival. DSO. MC.   - Awarded CROIX DE GUERRE avec etoile en Argent. 26.1.19.
Captain. R2L.V. Doake. DS O. MC.   -   "   "   "
2/Lieut. W. Tysoe. DSO. MC.   -   "   "   "

SPORTS:

18TH DIVISION KNOCK-OUT FOOTBALL COMPETITION - 1ST ROUND.
Battalion defeated 6th Bn. Northamptonshire Regt. 5 - 0
Battalion defeated 11th Bn. Royal Fusiliers.   3 - 0
Battalion defeated 18th Div. Royal Engineers.   3 - 0
Battalion defeated 8th Royal Berks.   4 - 1

WAR DIARY
or
INTELLIGENCE SUMMARY.

(Erase heading not required.)

Army Form C. 2118.

Place	Date	Hour	Summary of Events and Information	Remarks and references to Appendices
	4.2.19.		S P O R T S	

18TH DIVISIONAL KNOCK-OUT FOOTBALL COMPETITION.

    FINAL. Battalion defeated 18th Division Ammunition Column 1 - 0 and won the Division Cup.

XIII CORPS KNOCK-OUT FOOTBALL COMPETITION.

    1ST ROUND:. Battalion defeated Corps H.A. Team. - 5 - 2.

L/Cpl. GOUGH, 1st man of 18th Division home in Corps Cross-Country Race and awarded Div. Cross-Country Cup.

H.A. Knipe Major.

Commanding 2nd Bn. Bedfordshire Regiment.

WAR DIARY
~~INTELLIGENCE~~ SUMMARY.
(Erase heading not required.)

Army Form C. 2118.

Instructions regarding War Diaries and Intelligence Summaries are contained in F. S. Regs., Part II. and the Staff Manual respectively. Title pages will be prepared in manuscript.

Place	Date	Hour	Summary of Events and Information	Remarks and references to Appendices
SELVIGNY.	1. 2. 19		Brigade Ceremonial Parade - Presentation of Union Flags by Corps Commander. Brigade Dance in evening.	
	2. 2. 19		Lecture on Africa to the Brigade.	
	3. 2. 19		Inspection of battalions by C.O's.	
	4. 2. 19		Battalions at disposal of Battalion Commanders.	
	5. 2. 19		Bathing.	
	6. 2. 19		Route marches etc., under battalion arrangements.	
	7. 2. 19		Church Parade.	
	8. 2. 19		Lectures to Brigade on "New India", "Shaping the New World" etc.	
	9. 2. 19			
	10. 2. 19			
	11. 2. 19		Battalions at disposal of Battalion Commanders.	
	12. 2. 19			
	13. 2. 19		Bathing.	
	14. 2. 19		Games. Brigade Dance in the evening.	
	15. 2. 19		Church Parade.	
	16. 2. 19			
	17. 2. 19		Battalions at disposal of Battalion Commanders.	
	18. 2. 19			
	19. 2. 19			
	20. 2. 19		Bathing.	
	21. 2. 19		Games. Brigade Dance in the evening.	
	22. 2. 19		Voluntary Church Services.	
	23. 2. 19			
	24. 2. 19		Bathing.	
	25. 2. 19			
	26. 2. 19		Battalions at disposal of Battalion Commanders.	
	27. 2. 19			
	28. 2. 19			

Lieut. Colonel.
Commdg. 54th Infantry Brigade.

WAR DIARY or INTELLIGENCE SUMMARY.

(Erase heading not required.)

2nd Bn. Bedfordshire Regiment.

During the month of February 1919, the Battalion were billetted in SELVIGNY.

The Battalion was engaged in demobilization, training, etc.

On 17th February, 1919, the Battalion was inspected by General Officer Commanding 54th Infantry Brigade.

Lieut. S.W. Goble, M.C. proceeded to CAMBRAI for Demobilization on 5.2.19.
Lieut. W. Dayrell-Steyning proceeded to CAMBRAI for demobilization on 8.2.19.
Lieut. W.J. Holbrook, M.C. proceeded to CAMBRAI, for demobilization on 28.2.19.
2nd Lieut. A.S.A. Nixon, proceeded to CAMBRAI for demobilization on 28.2.19.
During the month of February 341 O.R. were demobilized.

The following Officers and 200 O.R. proceeded to join 11th Bn. Suffolk Regiment on 26.2.1919 for duty with Armies of Occupation.
2nd Lieut. L.S. ROWE.   2nd Lieut. C.P. MARRIS.   2nd Lieut. A.E. THOMAS.
2nd Lieut. W.K. HARDING.

No.15083 Sgt. H. Swannell awarded 2nd Bar to M.M. (Authy PEACE GAZETTE).

Sports:- The Battalion Beat the 1/8th R. Warwick Regiment at Football in the XIII Corps Knock-Out Football Competition, by 2 Goals to 1 on 17th Feb. 1919. The Battalion were defeated in the XIII Corps Competition by the Scottish Horse (50th Div) 4 Goals to 1 on 23.2.19.

3.3.19.   Commanding 2nd Bn. Bedfordshire Regiment.   Lt. Colonel

WAR DIARY
or
INTELLIGENCE SUMMARY.
(Erase heading not required.)

Army Form C. 2118.

Place	Date	Hour	Summary of Events and Information	Remarks and references to Appendices

	1st to 31st March 1919.		2nd Bn.Bedfordshire Regiment.
			――――000――――
			
			Battalion at SELVIGNY during the whole of the month, awaiting instructions for Cadre to proceed home and dispersal of retainable personnel.
			
			Lieut.W.J.Holbrook, M.C. and 2nd Lieut.A.S.A.Nixon proceeded to England for repatriation 28.2.19.
			Capt.A.F.Mackenzie joined Battalion 8.3.19.
			Capt.A.P.Methuen & Lieut.T.J.Pemberton proceeded to CAMBRAI for demobilization 8.3.19.
			Lieut.T.H.Flavell and 2nd Lieut.D.W.Boyd to CAMBRAI for demobilization 15.3.19.
			2nd Lieut.W.H.Ridgewell ――――――do――――――
			2nd Lieut.P.H.Lantley to CAMBRAI for demobilization 24.3.19.
			Lieut.H.B.Lang, M.C. proceeded on leave to CANADA on 30.3.19 and struck off strength.
			Capt.(Rev) B.B.Beard, Chaplains Department proceeded for demobilization 31.3.19.
			Capt.J.Thompson (R.A.M.C.) rejoined 54th Fd.Amb. on 8.3.19 and ceased to be attached.
			2nd Lieut.G.B.Phipps to England 30.3.19.
			2nd Lieut.R.J.Vince proceeded to join 92 Prisoners of War Company 10.3.19.
			36 Other Ranks demobilized during month of March.
			Bt.Major Act.Lt.Colonel A.E.Percival, D.S.O., M.C. granted temporary rank of Lt.Colonel under A.C.I.2 of 1919.
			
			7468 A/R.S.M. S.G.Armstrong, D.C.M. awarded Rumanian Decoration "CROIX de VIRTUTE MILITARA, 1st CLASS".
			
			                                                    Lt.Colonel
			                                      Commanding 2nd Bn.Bedfordshire Regiment.	

WAR DIARY
or
INTELLIGENCE SUMMARY.
(Erase heading not required.)

Army Form C. 2118.

2nd Bedfordshire Regiment.

During the month of April 1919, the Battalion was billeted in SEVIGNY.

Battalion returning "A" to progress home at Cadre strength.

Capt. L.I. Hawtrey, M.C., 2/Lt. Hyslop, 2/Lt. A. Waldock and a Draft of 80 Other Ranks proceeded to join 103 F.A. Company on 14.4.19.

A Draft of 80 Other Ranks was posted to 11th Bn. Suffolk Regiment on 13.4.19.

Lt.Colonel — Perceval, D.S.O., M.C. to U.K. 19.4.19. } To join Russian Volunteer
Capt. H. Prior, D.S.O., M.C. to U.K. 20.4.19. } Relief Force.
Capt. E. Clark, M.C. to U.K. 20.4.19
Capt. R. Bowles, M.C. to U.K. 20.4.19.

Lt. R.A.G. Brown to U.K. Sick 30.4.19.

Major L.H. Keep, D.S.O., M.C. assumed command of the Battalion 20.4.19.

J. Dixon, Major

Commanding 2nd Bedfordshire Regiment.

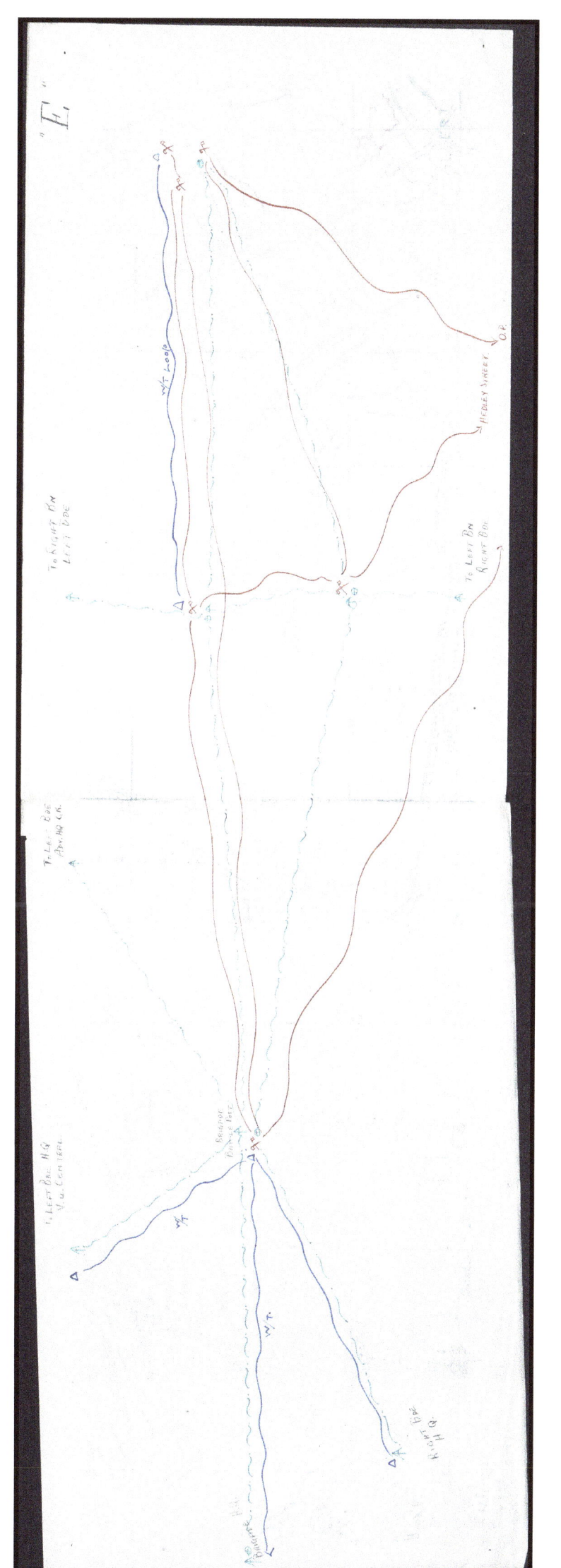

War Diary

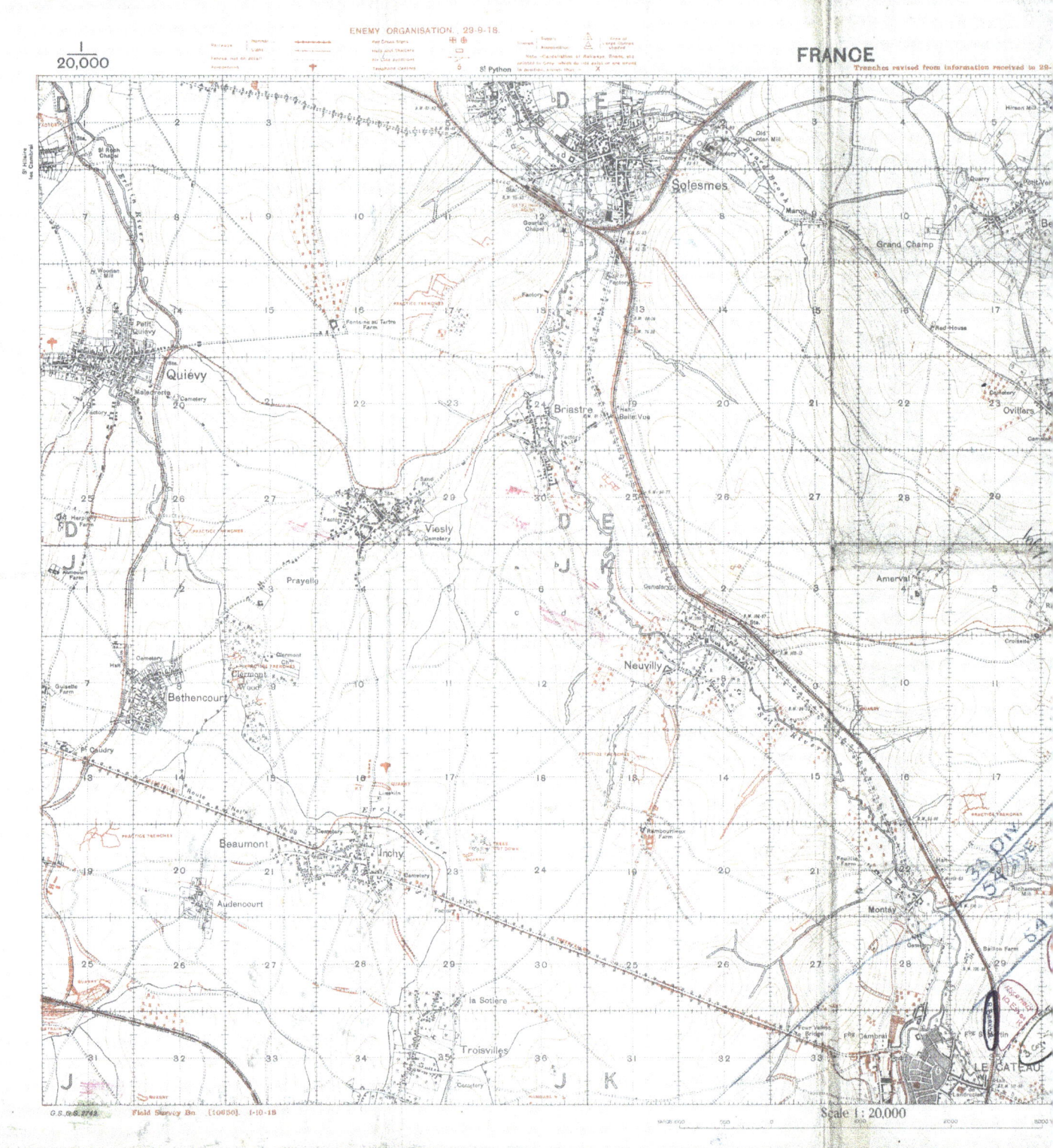

www.ingramcontent.com/pod-product-compliance
Lightning Source LLC
Chambersburg PA
CBHW081408160426

43193CB00013B/2132